ARABESQUE

AN ENGLISH INTERPRETATION

of

DUCHESSE LACE

with

DESIGN ADAPTATIONS FOR A VARIETY OF LACES

by

KAY BLAKEY

THE ELVISTON PRESS
YORK
ENGLAND

This book is dedicated to my husband, Fred, for his support and his help with the typing; to my son, Colin, for putting up with all the paperwork he found on every chair he tried to use; friends, Grace and Aileen, for reading through the text; Grace for working all the Carrickmacross patterns you see throughout the book; and especially for Dorothy and Ella, two very supportive dear friends who both died before the book was completed.

ARABESQUE
by Kay Blakey

ISBN 0 9522709 6 X

First published in the United Kingdom
by The Elviston Press 1999

© Kay Blakey 1999

British Library Cataloguing-in-Publication Data
A catalogue record for this book is available from the British Library.

The Elviston Press
Shiptonthorpe
York
England
YO43 3PB

CONTENTS

INTRODUCTION

Finally, after years of encouragement and urging by friends and students, I have consigned some of my collection of lace designs to print.

For years I have designed lace for my own use, for use by my friends, and for the instruction of my students. Once the decision to write the book was made, the difficulty was deciding which of the two hundred plus designs I had accumulated to include. Eventually I decided upon a selection for mixed abilities. Making the Duchesse lace took me two years - this gives you some idea of how long it will take if you decide to make every piece!

Having reached this stage, students and other lace teachers were showing interest in the designs, not only as Duchesse patterns but for different types of lace, and it soon became apparent that my English Interpretation of Duchesse lace was actually adaptable for many uses and applications, both in lace and embroidery. As you browse through the contents of the book, you will see some of the designs have already been interpreted in Needlelace, Carrickmacross and Honiton. The more adventurous lacemaker may like to try their hand at adaptations to Milanese lace or Withof or experiment with the use of colour. In each chapter you will see that I have included my ideas for fillings and braids when working other laces.

Finally, having said that the Duchesse lace takes two years to make, some of the designs may be made in a matter of days when worked in, say Carrickmacross - so please don't worry that my designs are a 'labour of love' - more a 'love of lace'!

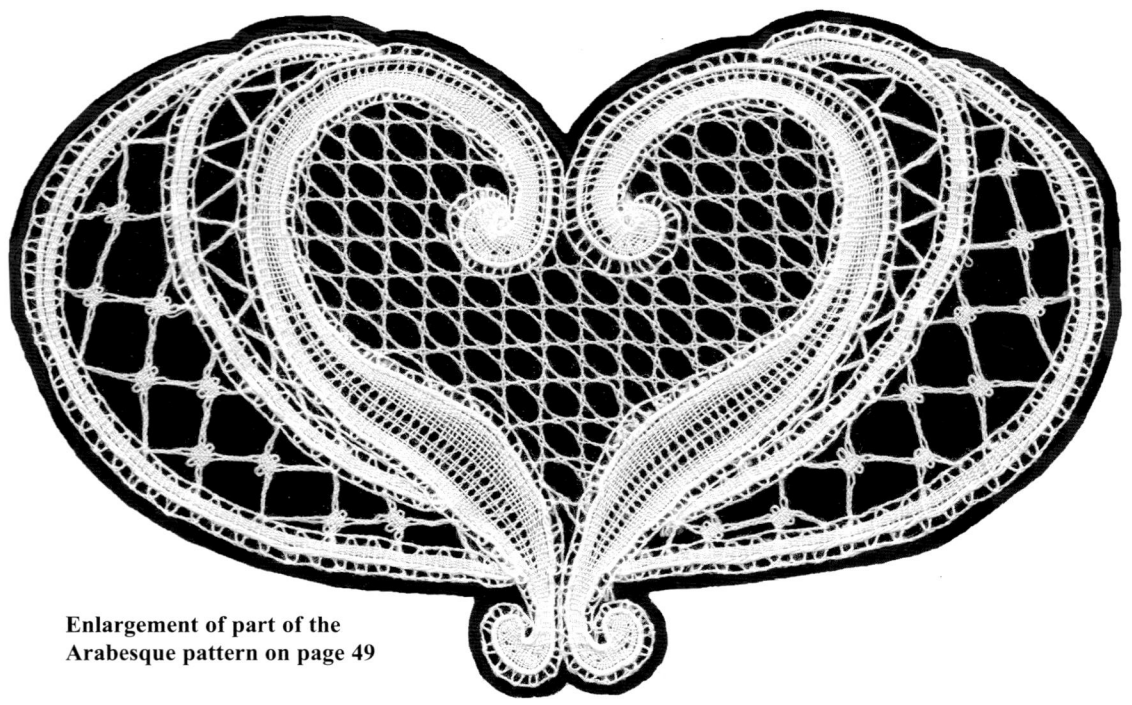

Enlargement of part of the Arabesque pattern on page 49

4

GENERAL INFORMATION

USING THE BOOK

Although each pattern in the book was originally designed for Duchesse lace, all the patterns are capable of being worked in a number of different laces. When starting a project, I feel it is best to have in mind the end use of the piece of lace, before deciding which type of lace to work.

The working instructions for each pattern refer to Duchesse Lace. The method for working the first pattern, 'Pearl Butterfly', is fully explained. In subsequent patterns you will be given the order of working along with any techniques not previously described. Instructions for starting and finishing Duchesse Lace and for the Duchesse fillings used in this book may be found on pages 7 - 17. Please remember to read fully all the instructions, from both the Techniques and Fillings chapters and the pattern itself, before starting a piece of work.

With some of the patterns, I have included examples of different laces along with ideas for others. The methods for many Duchesse techniques are similar when working Honiton, but I do suggest using your Honiton manual side by side with this book (and please experiment with the many beautiful Honiton fillings which may be found). Similarly, when making Carrickmacrosss and Needlelace please refer to your teachers' manuals. The Bibliography on page 64 refers to suitable books which may be of assistance.

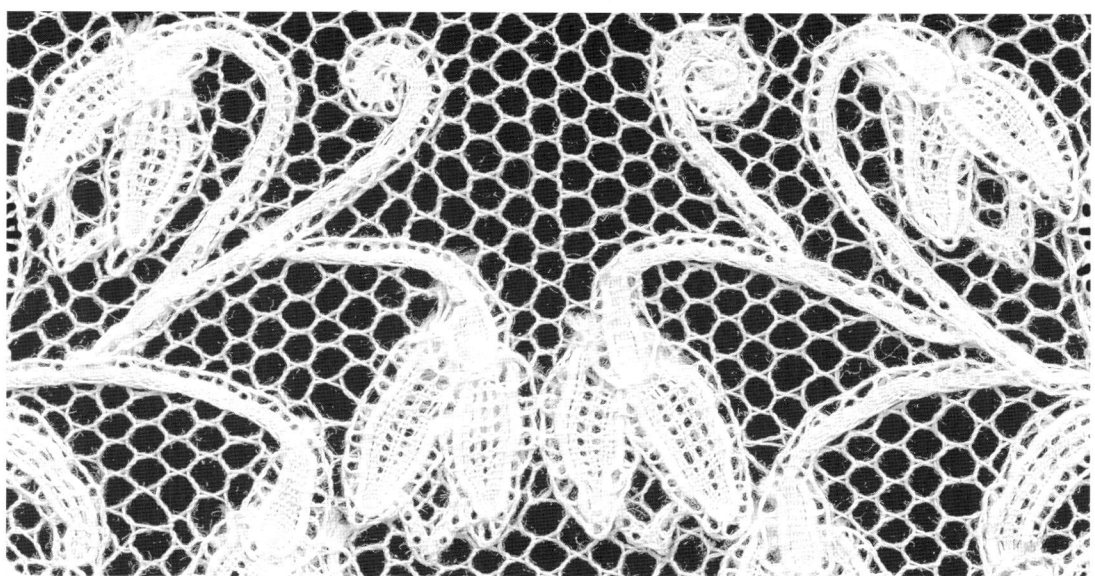

Enlargement of Jabot pattern (page 52)

Because of the versatility of the patterns, this book may be used by both beginners and advanced lacemakers (who have had the experience of tackling large pieces and have studied the various techniques).
My aim is for all lacemakers to use the patterns as a starting block, to develop their own ideas and interpretations.

THREADS AND MATERIALS

Unless otherwise stated, the following threads and materials were used when making up the patterns:

Duchesse   Egyptian Gassed Cotton 100/2 with DMC Coton a Broder 25 for the gimp.
NB I do feel that true Duchesse needs true egyptian cotton to get the nice smooth finish - other types of 100/2 cotton often 'fluff up' and become difficult to work with.

Needlelace   Egyptian Gassed Cotton 36/3 or Brok Cotton 36/3; couching down thread 120/2.

Honiton   Egyptian Gassed Cotton 120/2.

Carrickmacross   Cotton Organza; fine mesh Cotton Net; DMC Broder Machine 50.

PRICKING

Duchesse   Duchesse patterns have no pinholes shown on the pricking. The pattern is pricked as you work it, so that you can adjust the spaces where needed, depending on the size of the pin heads.

Honiton   Please remember that you **DO NOT** prick the fillings in the duchesse pricking; instead replace with your choice of filling.

GLOSSARY & ABBREVIATIONS

Gimp Companion Pair -
One bobbin is wound with a thick thread and one bobbin is wound with a thin thread; the bobbins are tied together and supported with a pin.

Double Gimp Companion Pair-
Wind a pair of bobbins with the thick thread and a pair of bobbins with the thin thread; lay the bobbins together open; support on a pin and use them to go down either side of a piece of lace, usually scrolls, braids and leaves. The thick thread is always on the outside unless otherwise stated.

Whole stitch -	cloth stitch	linen stitch	cr.tw.cr.
Half stitch -			cr.tw.
Double stitch -	cloth stitch and a twist		cr.tw.cr.tw.
Edge Stitch -	whole stitch and 2 twists		wh st.tw.tw.
Right Hand -	RH		
Left Hand -	LH		

DUCHESSE TECHNIQUES

STRAIGHT EDGE START

Working from the left, hang 4 pairs open on the first pin, then 2 on each of the following pins *(fig 1)*:

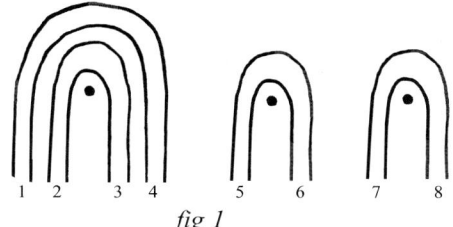

fig 1

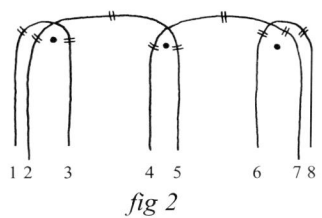

fig 2

With pairs 1 & 2, whole stitch and two twists, leave. Repeat with pairs 3 & 4 and pairs 4 & 5; take the right hand pair of the pairs just worked round the back of the pin, leave *(fig 2)*.

With pairs 6 & 7, work whole stitch and two twists; take the right hand pair round the back of the pin.

Continue this way until all the pairs are worked - this makes the top edge.

Now hang in the gimp companion pairs (that is one thick thread and one thin thread):

place support pins as shown *(fig 3)*; lay in one gimp companion pair two pairs from the left and another gimp companion pair one pair from the right.

Using the second pair from the left, work whole stitch across from left to right.

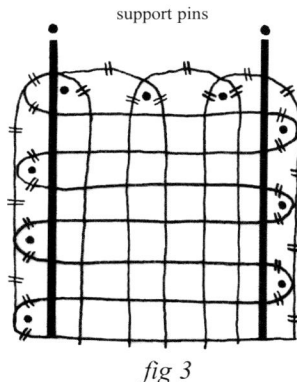

fig 3

NB If you are working in half stitch:

using the second pair from the left, work one whole stitch through the gimp companion pair and then change to half stitch - **do not twist** before you start the half stitch (this is done so there is no hole left showing).

Continue in half stitch to the edge pair; then whole stitch and two twists, pin, and work back. When working the gimp companion pairs in a section of half stitch, always remember to whole stitch through the gimp companion pair coming out to the edge and half stitch going back in.

POINT START

Hang 4 pairs open on the point pin **a** and 2 pairs on each of pins **b** and **c** (fig 4).

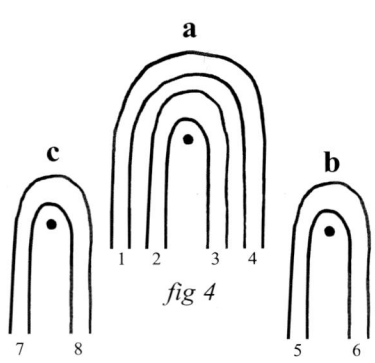

fig 4

Starting with the pairs on point pin **a**:
whole stitch and 2 twists with pairs 1 & 2 on the LH side, leave;
whole stitch and 2 twists with pairs 3 & 4 on the RH side, leave.

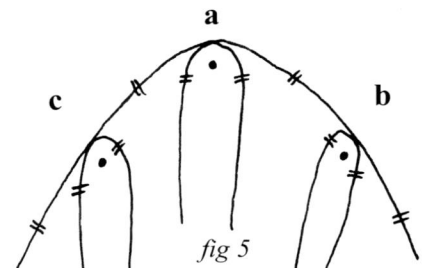

fig 5

With the RH pair at pin **a** (pair 4) and the LH pair at pin **b** (pair 5), whole stitch and two twists; take the RH pair of the pairs just worked round the back of pin **b**, leave (fig 5).

Repeat on the other side with the LH pair (pair 1) of pin **a** and the RH pair of pin **c** (pair 8).

Continue this way until all pairs have been worked.

A double gimp companion pair is added in a point start (fig 6). There are two methods of working the point:

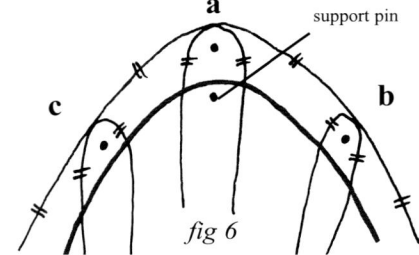

fig 6

Method A

Support the middle of the gimp companion pair on a temporary pin just under pin **a**; whole stitch through the pairs on either side, making sure the thick thread is on the outside (fig 7).

Take the RH pair just worked and whole stitch through the 2 pairs at **b**; repeat with the LH pair from **a** and the 2 pairs at **c**.

Taking the last pair worked at **c** as workers, whole stitch through 3 pairs; leave.

Take the last pair worked through as workers and work through to the outside edge at **d**, edge stitch, pin.

Continue working the pattern.

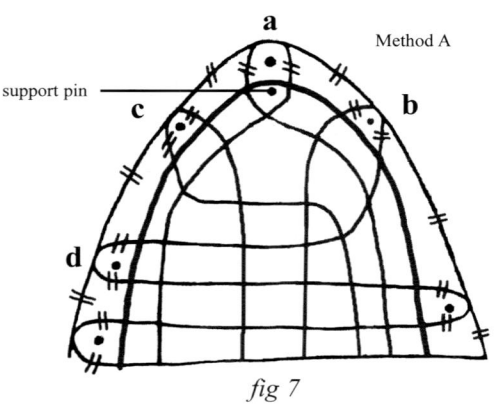

fig 7

Method B

Whole stitch together the 2 centre pairs at **a**.

Take the RH pair from **a** through both pairs at **b**; leave.

Taking the last pair worked through at **b** as workers, work to **c** (do not work through gimp companion pair); leave.

Taking the last pair worked through as new workers, whole stitch to the edge at **d** (including the gimp companion pair); edge stitch, pin.

Continue working the pattern.

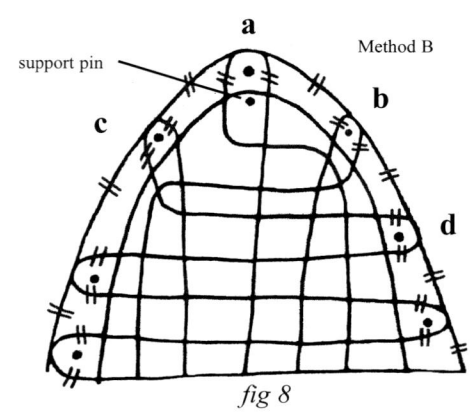

fig 8

8

SCROLL START (also known as a Curved Start)

Hang 4 pairs open on pin **a** and 2 pairs open on each of pins **b**, **c** and **d** *(fig 9)*.

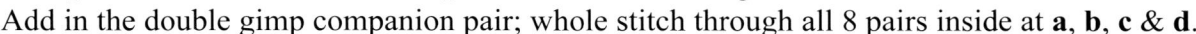

fig 9

Starting with the pairs on pin **a**, work whole stitch and two twists to make the edge in the same way as for a point start; continue until all pairs are worked through.
Add in the double gimp companion pair; whole stitch through all 8 pairs inside at **a**, **b**, **c** & **d**.

Now start working the scroll *(fig 10)*:
With the pairs from **a**, whole stitch through the pairs at **b** - **do not work through the gimp companion pair.**

NB Please make sure you refer to both diagram and instructions when working the scroll.

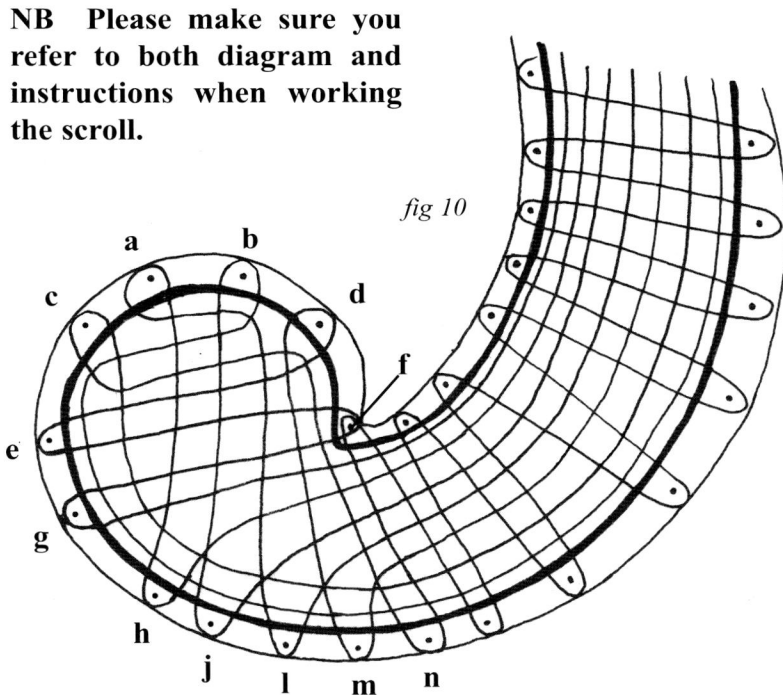

fig 10

Taking the last pair worked through at **b** as workers, whole stitch back through the pairs to **c** including the pairs coming from **c**; leave workers here (to become passives) and take the last pair worked as the new workers.
Whole stitch back to **d** including the pairs coming from **d**; leave workers here and take the last pair worked as the new worker pair. You should now have 10 pairs plus the gimp companion pair.
Whole stitch through **all** pairs (including the gimp companion pair) to **e**; edge stitch (whole stitch and two twists), pin;

work back to **f** (again including the gimp companion pair); edge stitch, pin; work back through to all pairs to **g**; edge stitch, pin;
whole stitch back through gimp companion plus 7 pairs until you reach the gimp companion pair on the RH side; leave workers here (to later become passives).
Take the 4th pair from the outer edge as workers, whole stitch back to the outer edge at **h; edge stitch, pin and work back through the gimp companion plus 6 pairs to where the last worker pair was left; leave this pair here. Repeat from ** for pins **j**, **l** & **m**, reducing the number of pairs worked through by one each time.
Take the last pair worked through, whole stitch to **n**, edge stitch, pin, work back to **f**, sew in.
Continue working the scroll braid.

SCROLL FINISH (Also known as a Curved Finish)

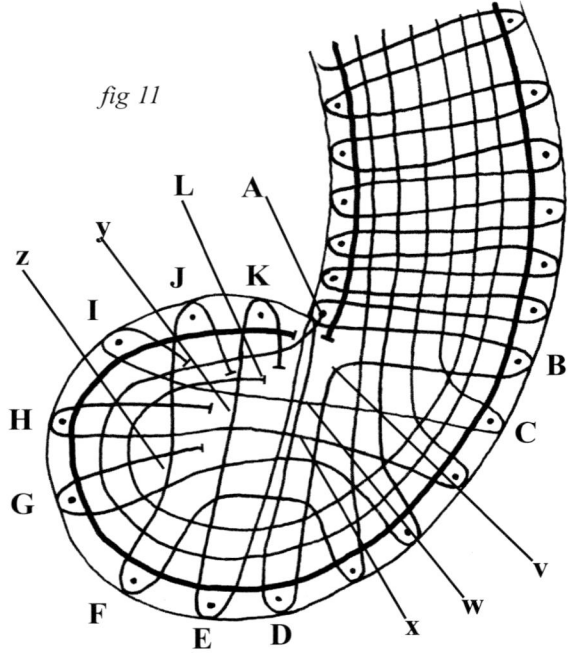

fig 11

NB Please make sure you refer to both diagram and instructions.

Work in whole stitch throughout the finish

Work to pin **A** *(fig 11)*; edge stitch, pin; throw out the gimp companion pair on this side.
Work back to pin **B**; edge stitch, pin; work through the remaining gimp companion and passive pairs; leave workers at **v**.

* Taking the fourth pair from the outside edge as workers, work to **C**; edge stitch, pin; work back through the passive pairs; leave at **w**.
Repeat from * until all but the last two passive pairs have been worked.
With the pair left at **v**, work to the edge at **D**, edge stitch, pin; work back through all the pairs to pin **A**; leave it here to be thrown out.
TURN PILLOW
Taking the edge pair at **A**, work through all passive pairs to **E**, edge stitch, pin; work back to **y**; leave.
Taking the fourth pair from the outside edge, work to the edge at **F**, edge stitch, pin; work back through 4 pairs to **z**; leave.
Taking the last pair worked through as the new workers, work out to the edge at **G**, edge stitch, pin; work back through 4 pairs and throw out.
Taking the 6th pair from the left edge, work to the edge at **H**, edge stitch, pin; work back through 4 pairs and throw out.
Take up the pair at **w**, work to the edge at **I**, edge stitch, pin; work back through 2 pairs and throw out.
Taking the pair left at **F**, work to the edge at **J**, edge stitch, pin; work back through 2 pairs and throw out.
Take up the passive pair left at **y**, work to the edge at **K**, edge stitch, pin; work back through 2 pairs and throw out.
With the 2 remaining passive pairs, sew the outer one in at **A**; throw out the last passive pair at **L**.
Throw out the gimp companion pair at **A**; sew an edge pair at **A**; tie off.
Carefully tie off all bobbins before cutting.

BRUGGE TIE

Sew all the pairs into their respective pinholes.
Starting with the first 2 bobbins on the right:
with the right hand bobbin make half a knot by
taking the right one over the left one *(fig12a)*;

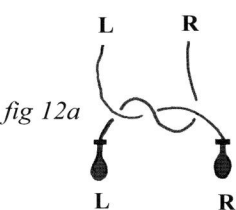

fig 12a

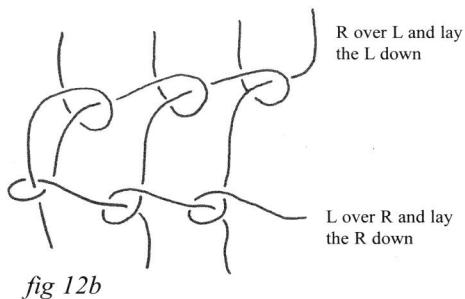

R over L and lay
the L down

L over R and lay
the R down

fig 12b

put down the bobbin which now comes into the left
hand; pick up the next bobbin on the left and work the
next knot; continue along the line to the end (right over
left and lay the left one down) *(fig 12b)*.
Return back along the line by working left over right and
lay the right one down.
Pull all the bobbins firmly before cutting off.

HANGING IN PAIRS

The new pair is hung on a support pin at the side of the work
(fig 13).
Lay it next to the gimp companion pair on the outside and work
a half stitch with it.
After a couple of rows, remove the support pin and gently pull
into place, taking care not to twist the threads.

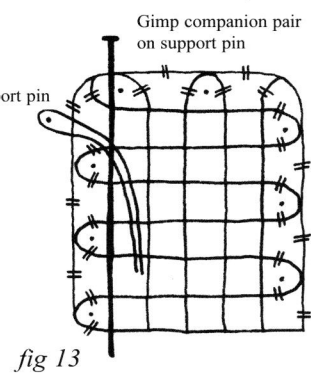

Gimp companion pair
on support pin

support pin

fig 13

DUCHESSE ROLL

This technique is used in 'Togetherness' *(page 33)*.
A 'roll' may be made with between 3 and 6 pairs depending on the thickness required - the
pairs used may include a gimp companion pair if required (Duchesse lace normally leaves
the gimp out of the roll, whereas Withof tends to include it). If you are working a small leaf
that only requires 6 pairs, reduce the number of pairs used in the 'roll'.

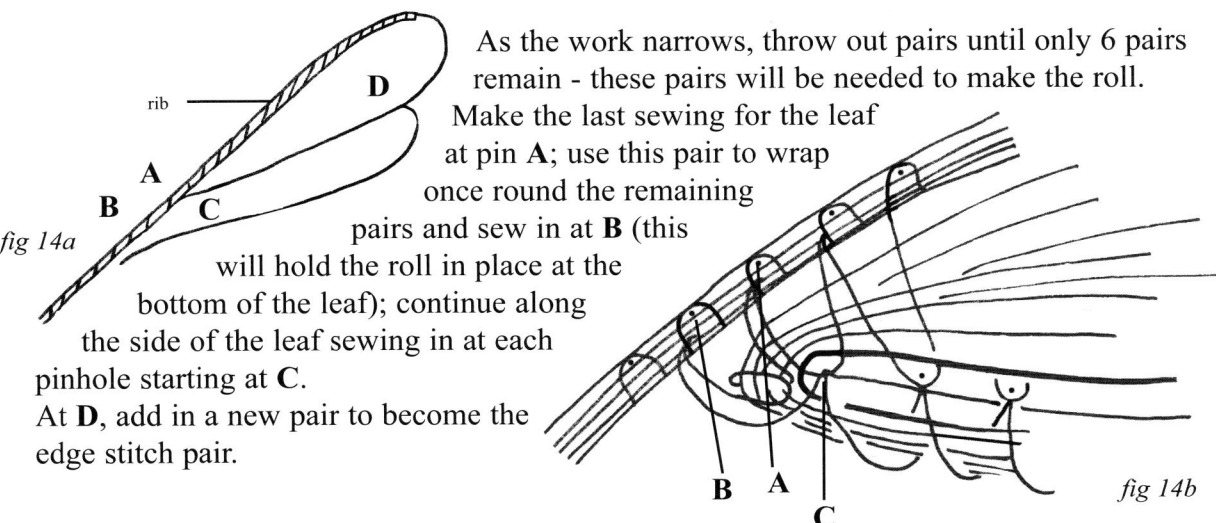

rib

D

A

B   C

fig 14a

As the work narrows, throw out pairs until only 6 pairs
remain - these pairs will be needed to make the roll.
Make the last sewing for the leaf
at pin **A**; use this pair to wrap
once round the remaining
pairs and sew in at **B** (this
will hold the roll in place at the
bottom of the leaf); continue along
the side of the leaf sewing in at each
pinhole starting at **C**.
At **D**, add in a new pair to become the
edge stitch pair.

B   A

C

fig 14b

FLOWER TECHNIQUES

TRANSFERRING PAIRS FROM ONE AREA TO ANOTHER

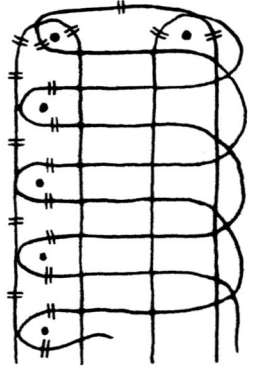

Using a straight start, work a rib of 6 pairs in the centre of the flower *(fig 15 & 16)*.
Join the rib by sewing the first 2 pairs into the first pinhole and the last 2 pairs into the other pinhole.
Work one row of a Brugge Tie *(fig 12b)*.

fig 15

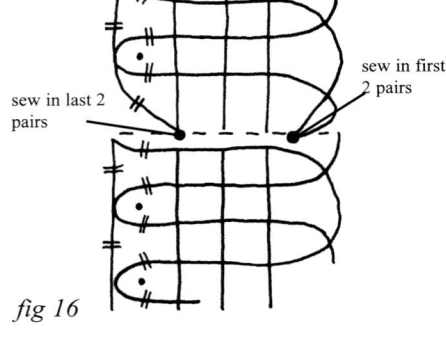

sew in last 2 pairs

sew in first 2 pairs

fig 16

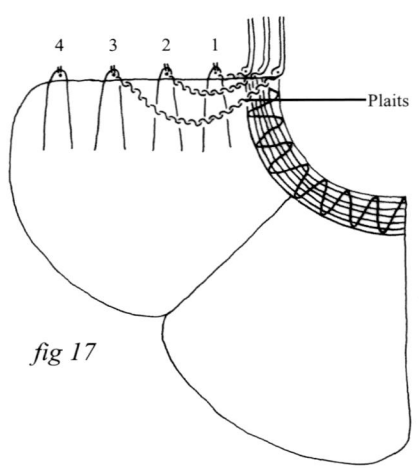

Plaits

fig 17

Start the transfer of the pairs from the rib to the petal by making 4 pinholes along the division of the petal *(fig 17)*.
Take pairs 1 & 2 and make a small plait to reach pin 1;
with pairs 3 & 4 make a plait to pin 2;
with pairs 5 & 6 make a plait to pin 3;
hang 2 extra pairs on pin 4;
add in a gimp companion pair.
The transfer of pairs is now complete.

BUNDLING ACROSS

(This technique is only used in the pattern, 'Arabesque' on *page 49*)
The bundle must be worked firmly and should **NOT** be visible on the right side of the finished piece of work.

To bundle pairs across from one petal to another, work the petal as normal until you reach the bottom of the petal.
Depending on the number of pairs in your petal: **either**
a)   every other pair is sewn into the centre of the flower; **or**
b)   sew in 1 pair, miss the next 2 pairs, sew in the next one and so on.

When all pairs have been sewn in:
starting from the left and paying close attention to the diagram *(fig 18)*,
take the first 4 pairs and use 1 of these pairs to wrap round the bundle;
*work along to the next pairs;
lay 2 pairs into the bundle along with the first wrapper pair and use the third pair as the new wrapper pair to continue wrapping round the bundle.
Repeat from * until you reach the end.

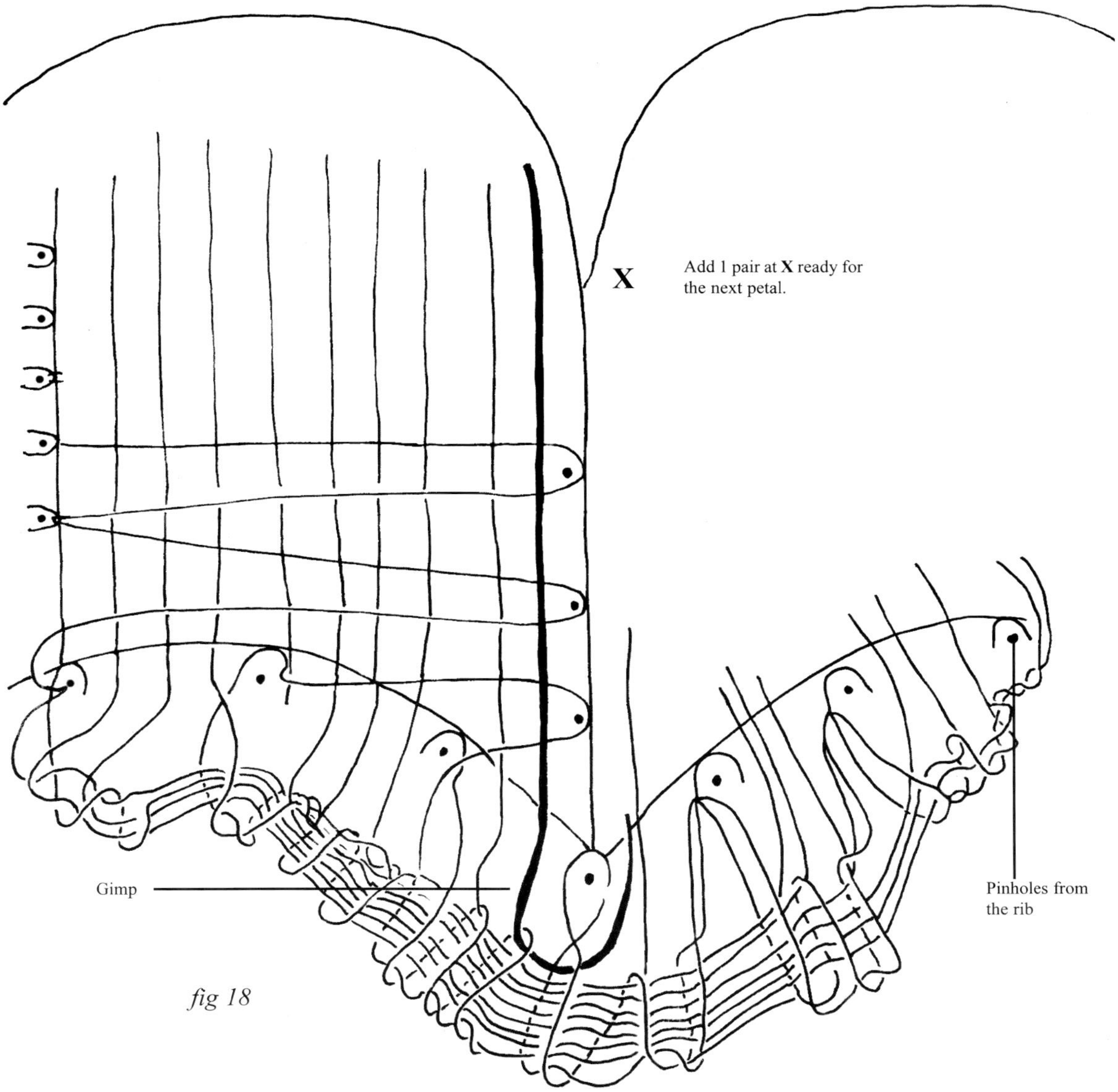

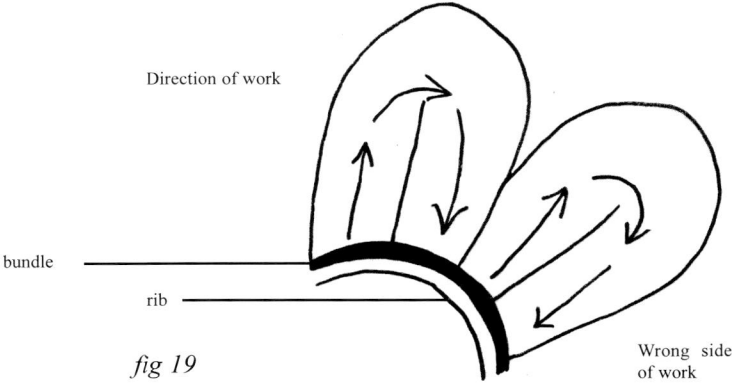

X Add 1 pair at **X** ready for
the next petal.

Gimp

Pinholes from
the rib

fig 18

Work across the bottom of the next petal, sewing in pairs and still working the bundle across, until all pairs have been evenly spaced along the bottom of the petal, ready to work the next petal *(fig 19)*.

Direction of work

bundle

rib

Wrong side
of work

fig 19

RIB PETAL FLOWER

Using 6 pairs, rib the centre of the flower and join. Transfer the pairs out to the petal at **A** *(fig 20)*; rib round the edge of the petal to **B**.

Work the last pinhole **B**, whole stitch through the passive pairs and make a sewing into the rib at the centre of the flower at **C**.

Work back through 2 pairs and leave the worker pair here.

With the last pair worked, whole stitch back to the centre and sew in.

Work back in whole stitch to the last pinhole **B**; take the working pair round the back of the pin, make an edge stitch and continue working the rib.

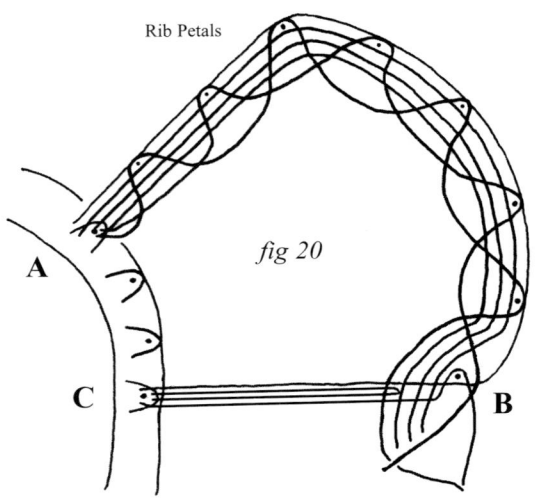

Rib Petals

fig 20

FLOWER PETAL DIVISION

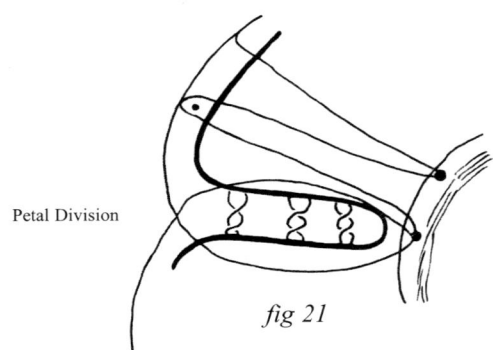

Petal Division

fig 21

Work the flower as normal until the division area is reached *(fig 21)*. Make sure that your working pair is at the outside edge.

Take the gimp companion pair and twist it once so that the thick thread is nearest to the centre.

With the gimp companion pair and the next pair, work a half stitch, put an extra twist on the LH pair; continue working through all the pairs until you reach the centre. **Do not sew in.**

Again, twist the gimp companion pair and work back in half stitch only (no extra twists), until the last 2 pairs are reached; whole stitch through the next pair and leave the gimp companion pair here.

With the last pair worked, work back to the centre and sew in.

Continue working the petal as normal.

HALF STITCH PLAIT IN FLOWER

Work the petal as normal until you reach pin **A** at the outside edge *(fig 22)*; edge stitch, pin.

Use the workers to work through the gimp companion pair and the 1st passive pair.

Then, using the 2nd passive pair and the workers, add a support pin at **B** and make a half stitch plait.

Before making the half stitch plait, lay back the remaining 4 pairs.

Work the half stitch plait to the centre; sew in; put back in place the 4 pairs previously laid back. Leave 1 pair from the plait at the centre and take the other pair as the worker pair.

Continue working the petal.

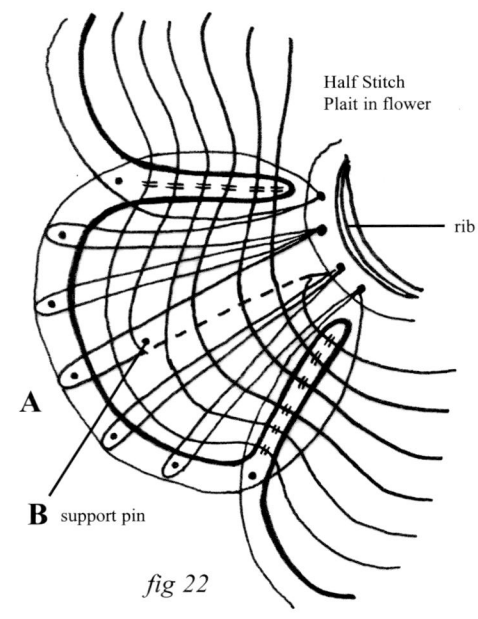

Half Stitch
Plait in flower

rib

A

B support pin

fig 22

DUCHESSE FILLINGS

The prickings in this section have been enlarged for clarity. To use as fillings for duchesse patterns, please reduce by 50%.

POINT GROUND

Sew in a pair opposite each pinhole.
Starting from the RH side of the work, take the first 2 pairs on the right,
* half stitch and two twists, pin; **do not** close the pin; leave the RH pair and pick up the next pair.
Repeat from *.

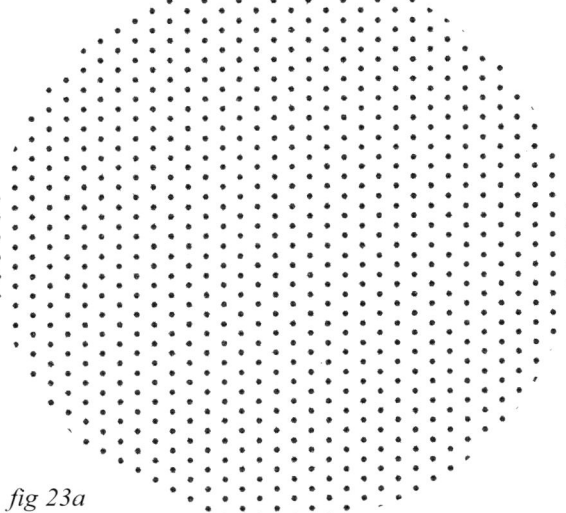

fig 23a

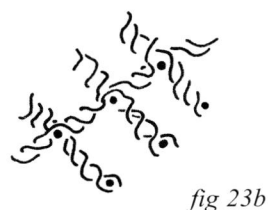

fig 23b

TORCHON HONEYCOMB GROUND (VARIATION)

This honeycomb is more oval in shape than the Midlands Honeycomb.
Sew in the required number of pairs at each pinhole opposite the pinhole to be worked.
The honeycomb is made up of one long row, followed by one short row.

LONG ROW (working from left to right): half stitch, pin, half stitch and twist; repeat this along the row.

SHORT ROW:
take the first 2 pairs and work
* half stitch, pin, half stitch and twist; leave*.
Pick up the next 2 pairs and repeat from * to *. Continue in this way working one long row and one short row until the filling is complete.

fig 24a

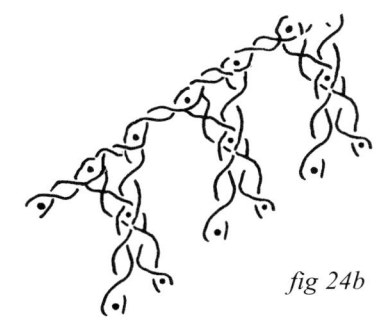

fig 24b

SNOWFLAKE

Each snowflake is worked in the same way.

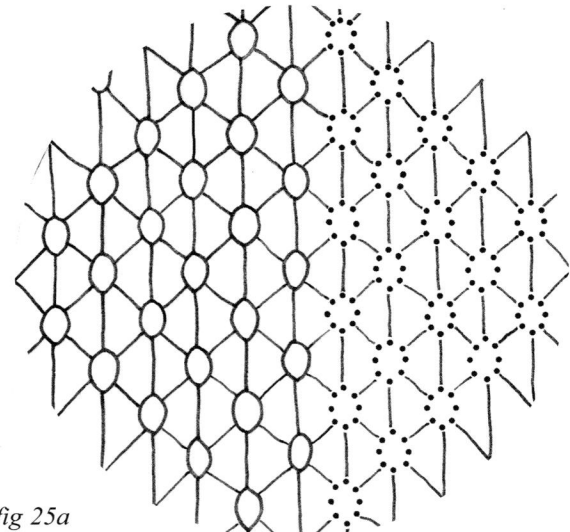

fig 25a

Sew in 2 pairs at the top of each line; make a small plait down to the oval shape.

Put a pin in at the bottom of each plait; twist each pair twice; take the first pair from the LHS and work through in whole stitch to the right; leave worker pair.

Taking the last pair worked as the new workers, whole stitch back to the left, twist workers twice, pin; work back to the right, twist workers twice, pin; whole stitch back to the left, twist workers twice, leave the workers here, pin.

Taking the last pair worked as the new workers, whole stitch back to the right, twist workers twice, pin, leave worker pair.
Taking the last pair worked, twist twice and make a plait with the old workers.
With the middle 2 passives, put a pin in; twist twice and make a plait with them.
Twist the remaining passive pair twice and make a plait with the remaining pair of old workers on the left.

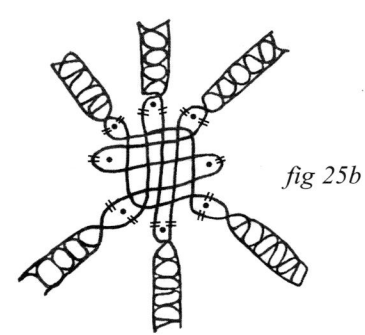

fig 25b

Larger snowflakes have an extra row in the middle.

LATTICE

This filling is worked from left to right with one pair working right across.

Sew in a pair opposite each pinhole.
Taking the first 2 pairs on the right,
*half stitch, pin, half stitch and two twists;
leave the RH pair and pick up the next pair.
Repeat from *.

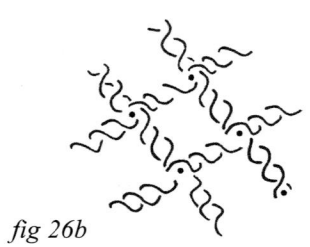

fig 26b

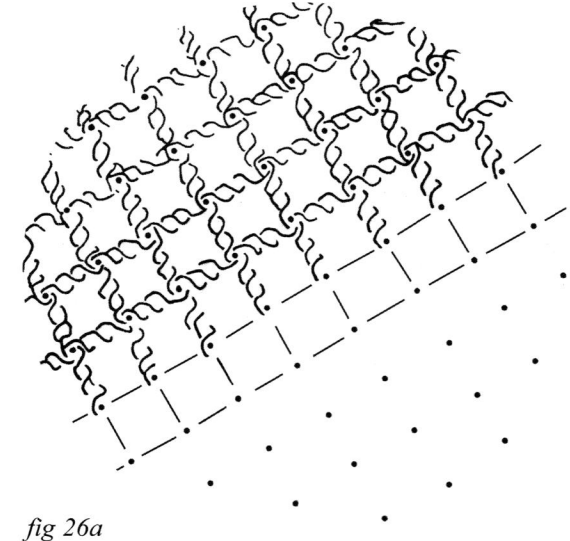

fig 26a

16

WHOLE STITCH BLOCK

Each block is made with 4 pairs and worked using the same method.

Sew in 2 pairs at each pinhole opposite the block to be worked. Plait the pairs down to the block. Put a pin at the end of each plait and twist each pair twice.

With the LH pair, whole stitch through to the right; leave this pair.

Taking the last pair worked through as workers, work back in whole stitch, twist twice, pin.

Whole stitch back to the right, twist twice, pin.

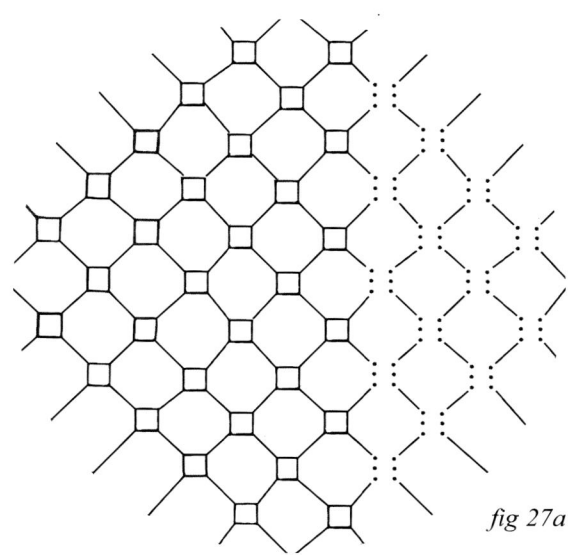

fig 27a

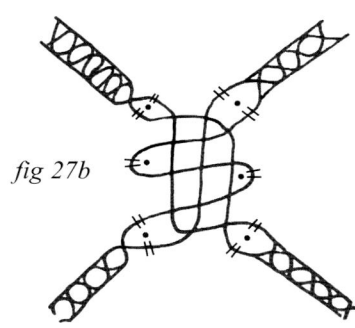

fig 27b

Whole stitch back to the left, twist twice, pin; leave this pair.

With the last pair worked through, whole stitch back to the right; twist twice; leave.

Twist the last pair worked through twice and make a plait with the worker pair.

With the 2 pairs on the left, twist the passive pair twice and make a plait with them.

BUCKS HONEYCOMB GROUND

This honeycomb is more rounded in shape.

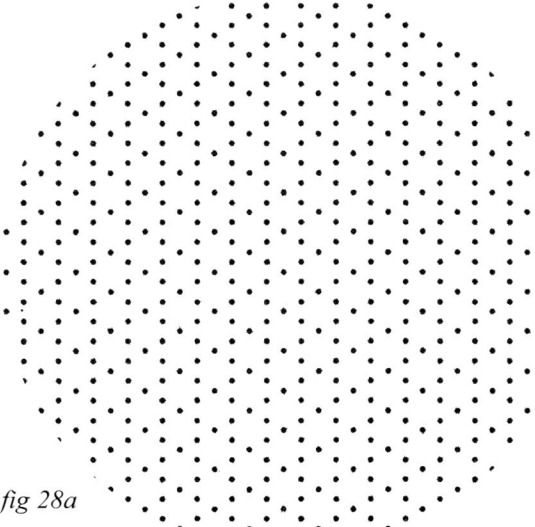

fig 28a

Sew in the number of pairs required opposite each pinhole to be worked.

The honeycomb is made up of one long row followed by one short row.

Long Row: Taking the first 2 pairs, half stitch and twist, pin, half stitch and twist.

Repeat along the row taking one pair completely across the row.

Short Row: This row is made working 2 pairs individually [half stitch and twist, pin, half stitch and twist], then leaving these 2 pairs, taking the next 2 pairs and repeating the stitch.

VARIATION - If you would like a much softer variation using this grid pattern, work each pinhole [half stitch, pin, half stitch and twist]. This makes the 'round' not as tight.

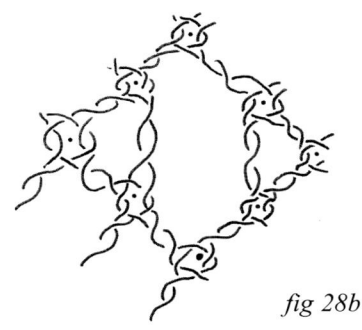

fig 28b

PEARL BUTTERFLY

The original pattern for this chapter was a simple string of pearls and flowers to go round a handkerchief edge. After thinking about it for some time I decided that the Pearl Butterfly would be more interesting to make. As you can see from the illustrations, the Pearl Butterfly is also extremely attractive when worked in Carrickmacross and Needlelace.

DUCHESSE FILLINGS
Point Ground
Tallies

You will need approximately 20 pairs Duchesse bobbins, 1 gimp companion pair, 1 double gimp companion pair, plus extra pairs for the fillings.

LARGE FLOWER

Working from the centre outward, start at 'A' *(fig 29)*.
Using a straight edge start *(page 7)*, make a 6 pair rib round the centre of the flower; complete the rib at **A** by sewing in and doing one row of Brugge Tie.

Take the first 2 pairs and make a very small plait, then put a pin in between them up the side of the petal.
Take the next 2 pairs and make the plait a bit longer, pin up next to the first pin.
Repeat from * to * for the last 2 pairs.
You will need to add another 4 pairs:
put in two more pins, making sure that the last pin is where each petal meets at the top;
on the pin next to the plaited pairs hang 2 pairs open, twist each pair twice;
on the top pin hang the remaining 2 pairs open, twist both pairs twice, then whole stitch with them.
Next, using a support pin, hang in a gimp companion pair.
From the centre, work the gimp companion pair in whole stitch through 9 passive pairs, leave.
The last pair worked is now the worker pair: work it back to the centre, working the first 2 passive pairs in whole stitch, the rest in half stitch.

Sew in the rib.
Work back in half stitch to the last 2 pairs before the gimp pair; change to whole stitch and work through the next three pairs; then,
[twist workers twice, pin, whole stitch with the last pair, twist both pairs twice] - this is the edge stitch; work back to the centre.
This now sets the pattern for the petal, the gimp making the division for each petal.

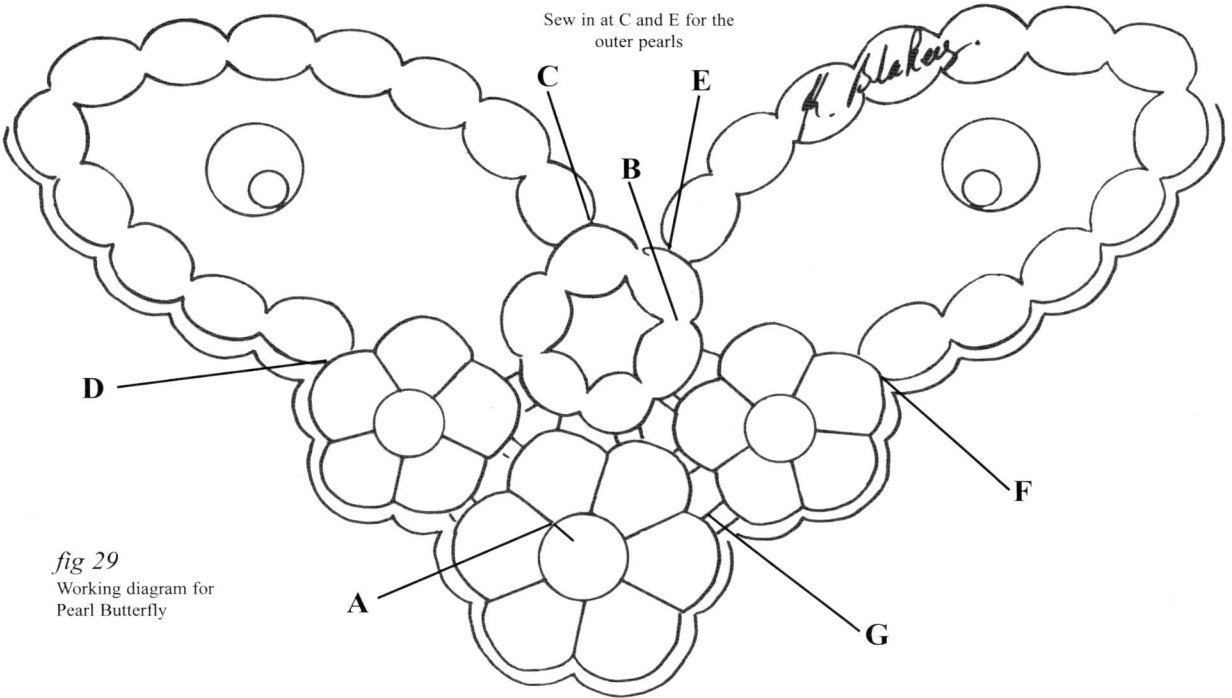

Sew in at C and E for the
outer pearls

C

E

B

D

F

A

G

fig 29
Working diagram for
Pearl Butterfly

DIVISION

Leave the worker pair on the outside edge.

Twist the gimp pair once; work the first 2 passive pairs in whole stitch, twist both pairs twice; work the remaining passives to the centre in half stitch, with an extra twist on each left hand bobbin. **Do not sew in.**

Twist the gimp pair again; work back in half stitch through the next 6 pairs; whole stitch the next 3 pairs; leave the gimp companion pair here.

The last pair worked through is now the worker pair.

Work back to the centre in pattern *[make up the edge, whole stitch gimp pair, 2 whole stitches, 6 half stitches]; sew in.

The division for each petal is the same.

Continue working each petal in the same pattern as *.

When the last petal has been worked, work the gimp pair out to the centre, leave.

Sew in 2 pairs of passives to each pinhole; tie off with a Brugge Tie, including the thin thread from the gimp pair; cut off all the bobbins.

This completes the flower.

SMALL FLOWER

The small flower starts with a rib using the same method as the large flower and is worked in the same way up the petal, except that at this stage, only 3 extra pairs and the gimp companion pair are added.

The small flower is worked in whole stitch with a twisted centre section of 3 pairs.

Work each petal with a gimp companion pair making the division; complete with a Brugge Tie; also, make a sewing into the large petal at **G** (where the small Bars are shown).

19

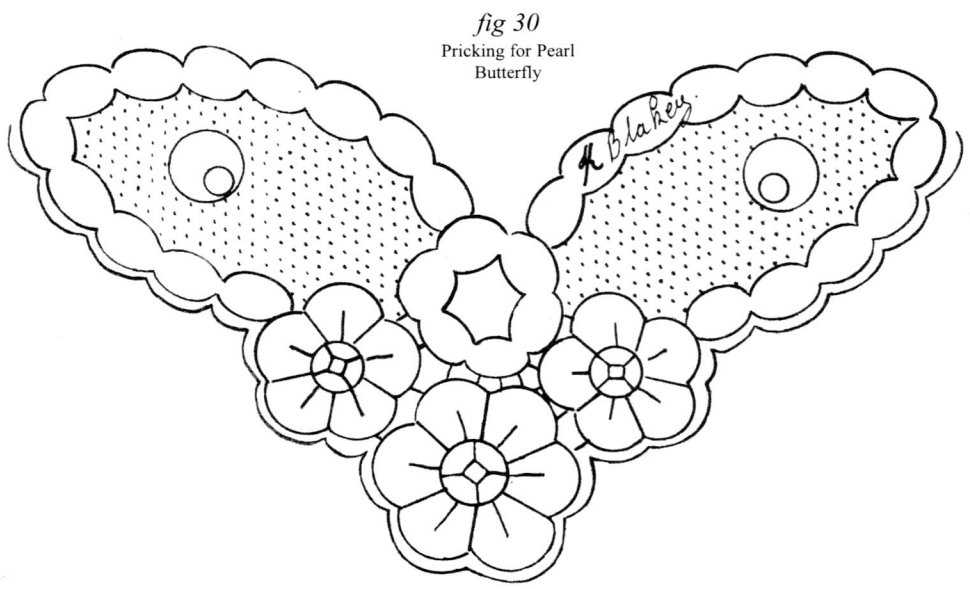

fig 30
Pricking for Pearl
Butterfly

BERRIES

Using 6 pairs start at **X** *(fig 31)* and rib to **Y**; add in a gimp companion pair at **Y** on the outside edge.

Work across to **Z**; edge stitch, increase to 10 pairs in total.

Work the berry in whole stitch, with twists added to make a pattern of your own choice. Decrease pairs so that when you reach starting point **X** there are only 6 pairs left; throw out the gimp pair; sew in the remainder; make a Brugge Tie.

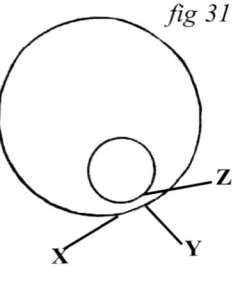

fig 31

CARRICKMACROSS FILLING
Triple Dot

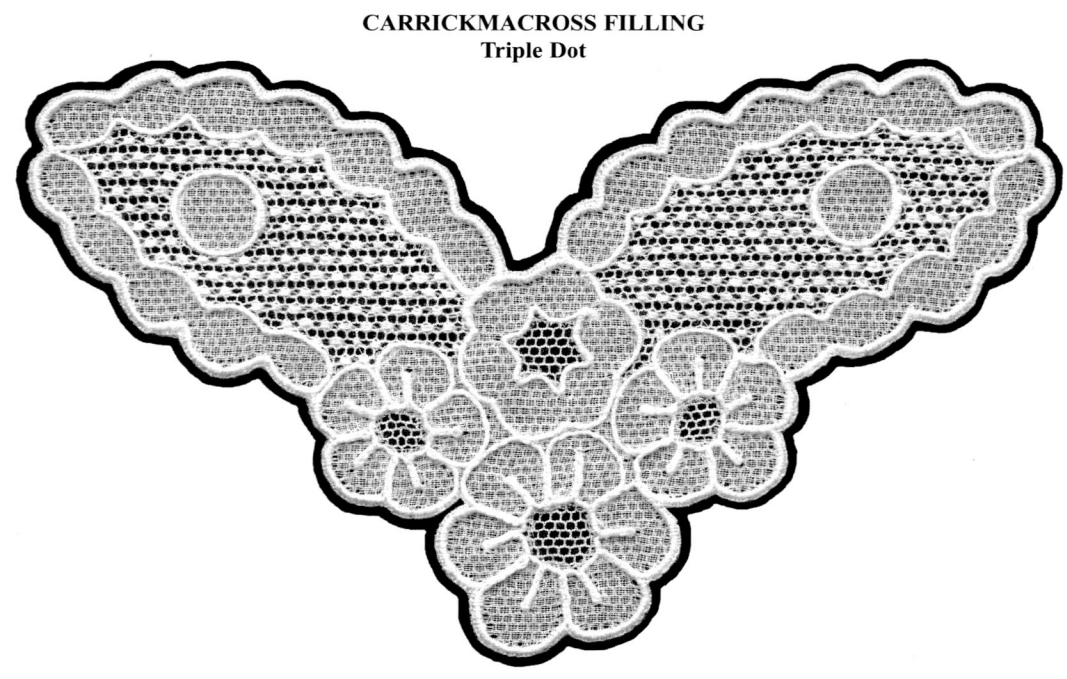

20

PEARLS

The pearls are worked in the simplest form with 8 pairs and a double gimp companion pair. Straight edge start at **B** *(fig 29)*.

Work each pearl in half stitch and use the gimp companion from the inside to make the division between each pearl.

Continue in this way until the circle is complete.

Cross the gimp threads and sew out the remaining pairs at the straight start.

OUTER PEARLS

Sew 8 pairs into the circle of pearls at **C** *(fig 29)*; add the double gimp companion pair.

Again, work in half stitch making the division as in the circle and sew out into the flower at **D**; finish with a Brugge Tie. Repeat for the Pearls from **E** to **F**.

The filling for the oval of pearls is point ground. Each flower has a tally in the centre.

PICOTS

The Picots are purely optional.

The outer line indicates where the picots may be made on the flowers and pearls.

NEEDLELACE FILLINGS
Pea Stitch
Twisted Buttonhole Stitch
Corded Brussels with Holes
Spider Web Wheel
Triple Brussels

ROSE-O-LEE

Our wild flowers are often forgotten, but this pretty edging was inspired by the simple but pretty shape of the Rosa Canina (Dog Rose). The pointed oval leaf shape is reflected in the corner design.

The full edging is worked in Duchesse, but if you wish to make just the corner, the pattern is suitable for both Carrickmacross and Needlelace.

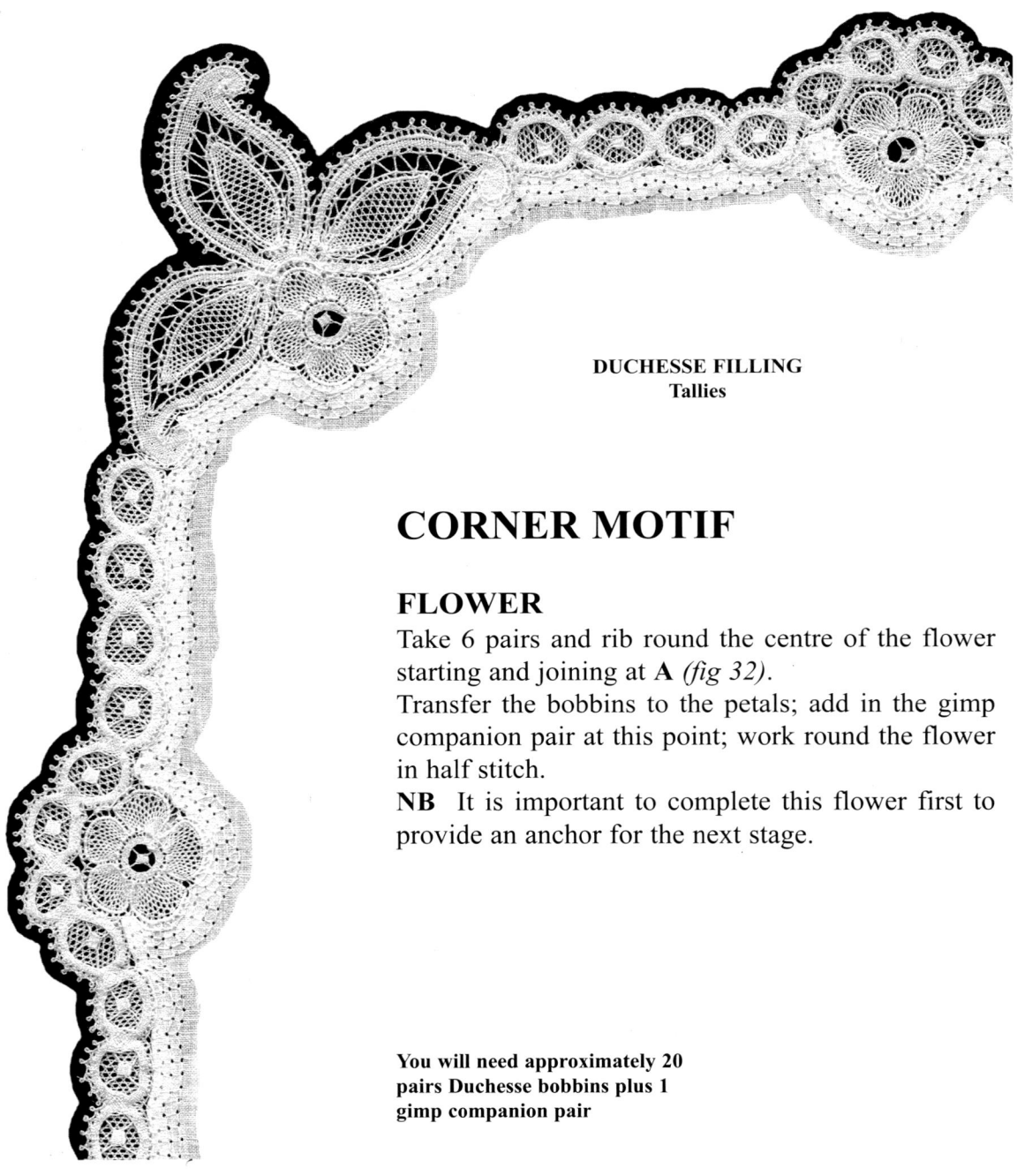

DUCHESSE FILLING
Tallies

CORNER MOTIF

FLOWER

Take 6 pairs and rib round the centre of the flower starting and joining at **A** *(fig 32)*.

Transfer the bobbins to the petals; add in the gimp companion pair at this point; work round the flower in half stitch.

NB It is important to complete this flower first to provide an anchor for the next stage.

You will need approximately 20 pairs Duchesse bobbins plus 1 gimp companion pair

CENTRE LEAF

Take 8 pairs and the double gimp companion pair to start a scroll at **B**, working in whole stitch; add in the extra pair as required for the division at **C**.

Do not forget to do the picots on the outside edge.

Divide the pairs for each side.

At **C** add in 2 extra pairs to form the new edge in the centre.

Continue in whole stitch until you reach **D**; join; work on, removing pairs as the leaf narrows; sew the remainder into the flower.

At **E**, make a point start using 6 pairs plus the gimp pair; work in half stitch adding in extra pairs of bobbins as the leaf widens and removing pairs as the leaf narrows, ending with 5 pairs plus the gimp pair; sew into the scroll edge.

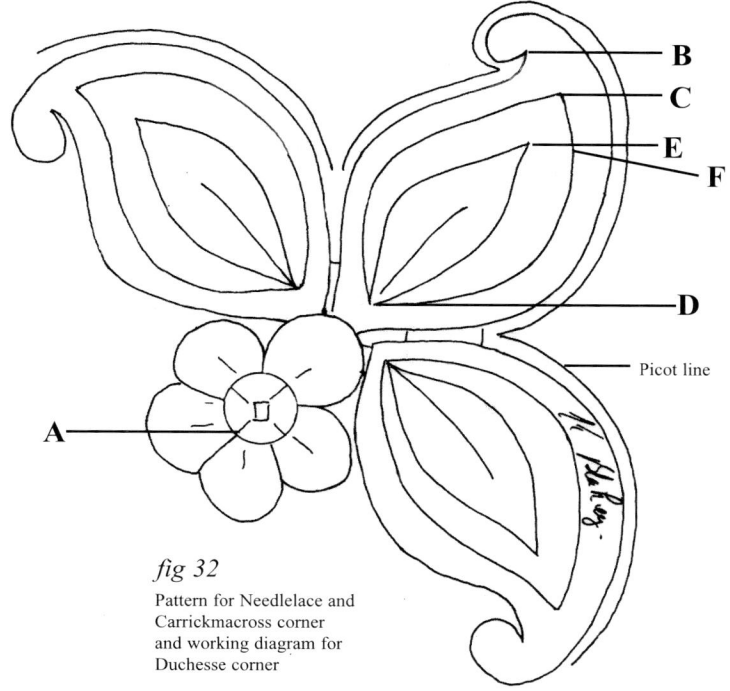

fig 32

Pattern for Needlelace and Carrickmacross corner and working diagram for Duchesse corner

Using 1 pair, join at **C**; twist pair three times then sew in at **E**; twist three times again and sew in at **F**.

Continue in this way to **D**, going backwards and forwards in a zig-zag; finish off.

Rejoin at **E** and complete the other side.

The remaining two leaves are both worked using the same method.

The flowers in the centre of each edge are all worked using the same method as the flower in the leaf corner. I found that if I worked the flowers before the beads, there was a nice firm edge to sew into.

CARRICKMACROSS FILLING
No filling used

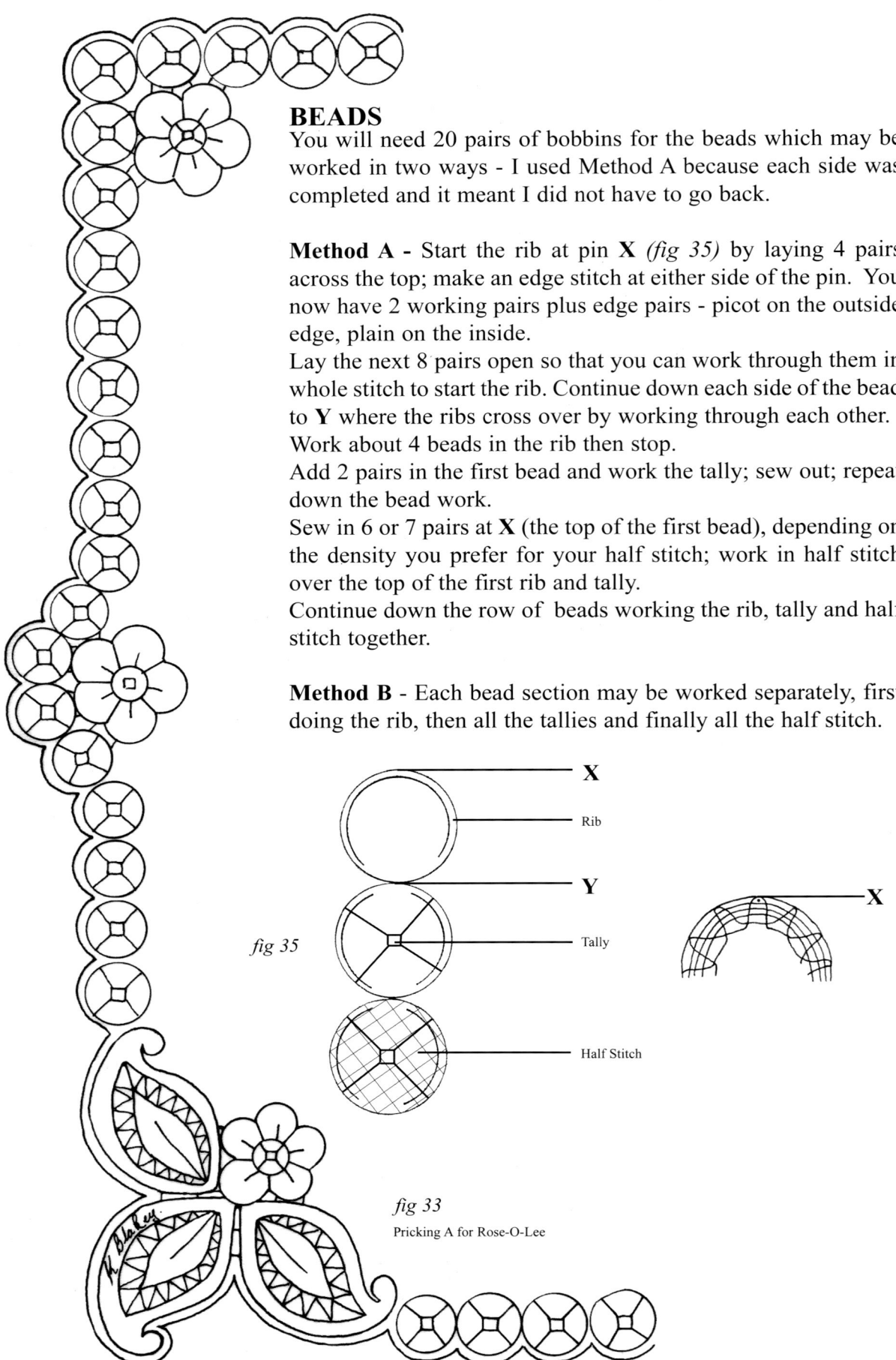

BEADS

You will need 20 pairs of bobbins for the beads which may be worked in two ways - I used Method A because each side was completed and it meant I did not have to go back.

Method A - Start the rib at pin **X** *(fig 35)* by laying 4 pairs across the top; make an edge stitch at either side of the pin. You now have 2 working pairs plus edge pairs - picot on the outside edge, plain on the inside.

Lay the next 8 pairs open so that you can work through them in whole stitch to start the rib. Continue down each side of the bead to **Y** where the ribs cross over by working through each other. Work about 4 beads in the rib then stop.

Add 2 pairs in the first bead and work the tally; sew out; repeat down the bead work.

Sew in 6 or 7 pairs at **X** (the top of the first bead), depending on the density you prefer for your half stitch; work in half stitch over the top of the first rib and tally.

Continue down the row of beads working the rib, tally and half stitch together.

Method B - Each bead section may be worked separately, first doing the rib, then all the tallies and finally all the half stitch.

X

Rib

Y

Tally

X

fig 35

Half Stitch

fig 33

Pricking A for Rose-O-Lee

24

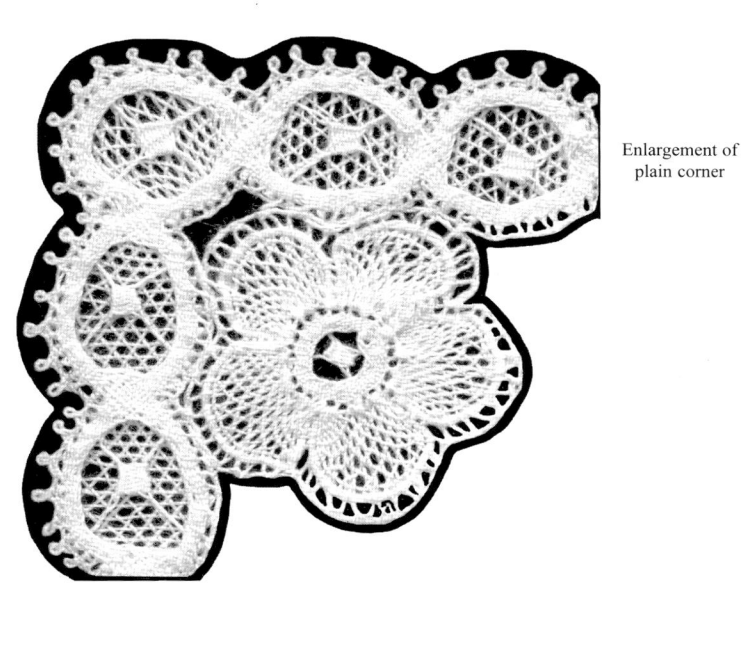

Enlargement of
plain corner

fig 34
Pricking B for Rose-O-Lee

To match prickings A & B *(figs 33 & 34)*:
on each side (without fancy corner), there are a total of 22 beads, 11 from corner to centre flower *(fig 34)*; from the fancy corner to the centre, there are 6 beads.

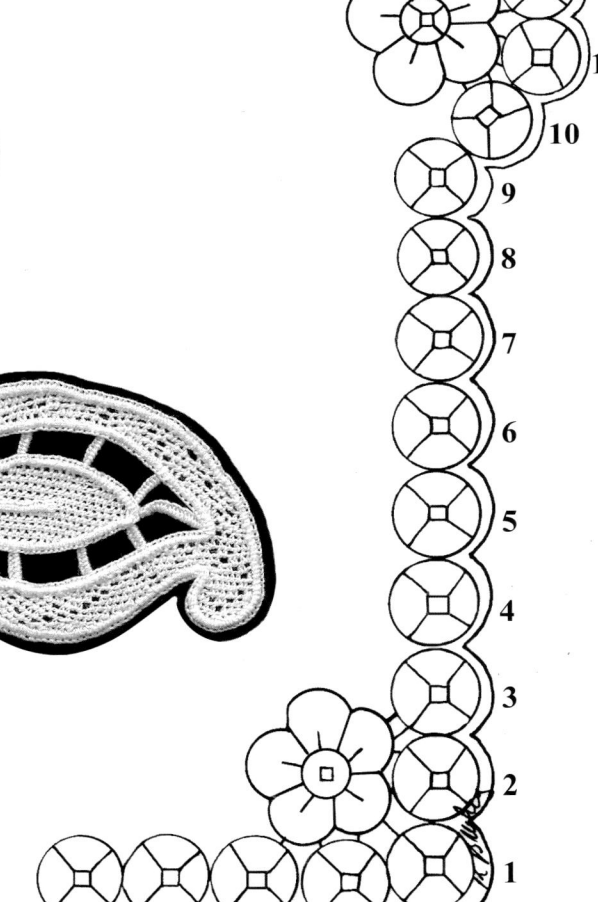

5
6
7
8
9
10
11
11
10
9
8
7
6
5
4
3
2
1

NEEDLELACE FILLINGS
Scrolls: Corded Brussels with Diagonal holes
Flower: Double Brussels
Spider Web Wheel
Leaves: Corded Brussels

5   4   3   2   1

CLOVER ROSE

his is a fairly simple Duchesse edging for a medium sized handkerchief, which should not take too long to make.

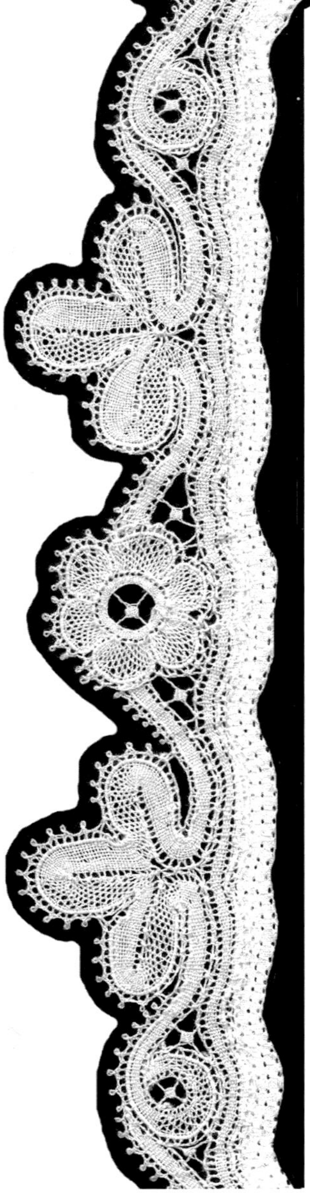

DUCHESSE FILLING
Tallies

You will need approximately
12 pairs Duchesse bobbins
plus 1 gimp companion pair.

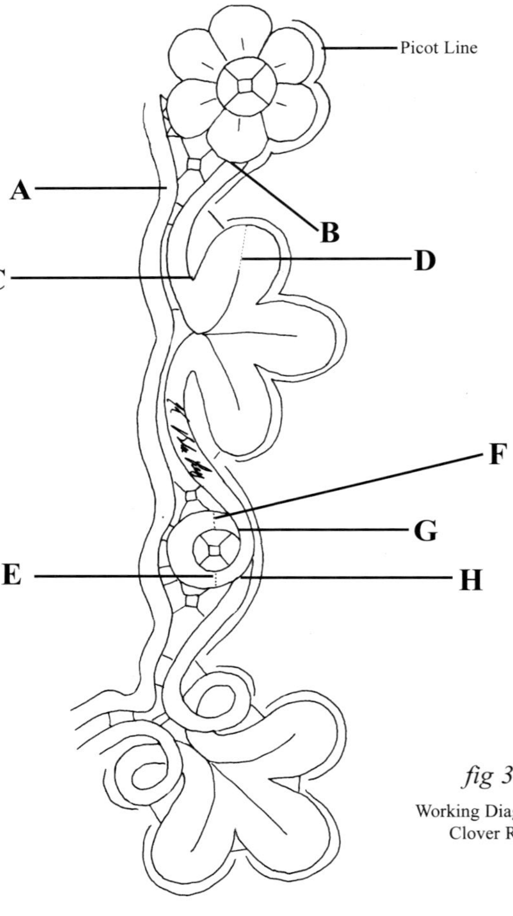

Picot Line

A

B

C

D

E

F

G

H

fig 36

Working Diagram for
Clover Rose

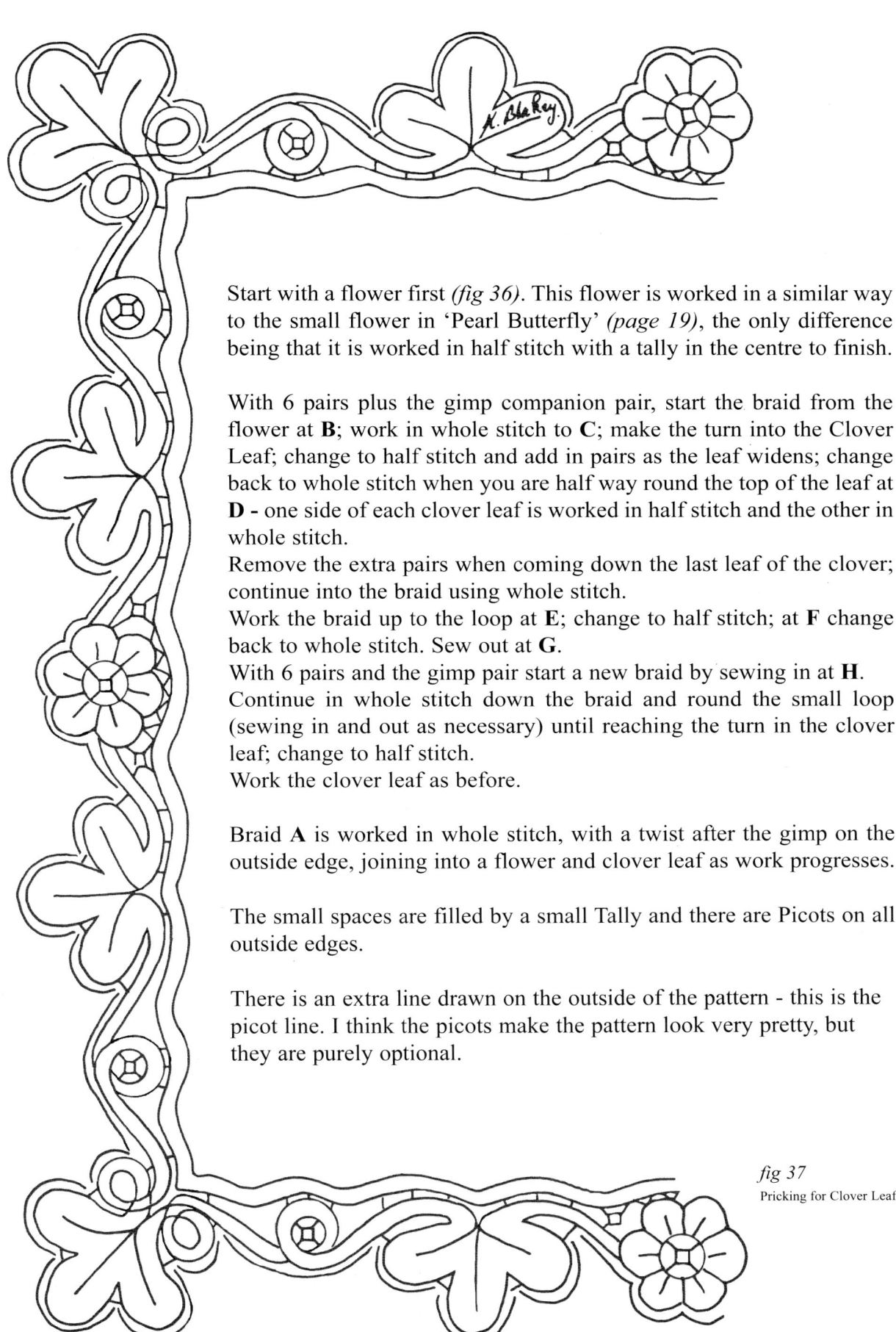

Start with a flower first *(fig 36)*. This flower is worked in a similar way to the small flower in 'Pearl Butterfly' *(page 19)*, the only difference being that it is worked in half stitch with a tally in the centre to finish.

With 6 pairs plus the gimp companion pair, start the braid from the flower at **B**; work in whole stitch to **C**; make the turn into the Clover Leaf; change to half stitch and add in pairs as the leaf widens; change back to whole stitch when you are half way round the top of the leaf at **D** - one side of each clover leaf is worked in half stitch and the other in whole stitch.
Remove the extra pairs when coming down the last leaf of the clover; continue into the braid using whole stitch.
Work the braid up to the loop at **E**; change to half stitch; at **F** change back to whole stitch. Sew out at **G**.
With 6 pairs and the gimp pair start a new braid by sewing in at **H**.
Continue in whole stitch down the braid and round the small loop (sewing in and out as necessary) until reaching the turn in the clover leaf; change to half stitch.
Work the clover leaf as before.

Braid **A** is worked in whole stitch, with a twist after the gimp on the outside edge, joining into a flower and clover leaf as work progresses.

The small spaces are filled by a small Tally and there are Picots on all outside edges.

There is an extra line drawn on the outside of the pattern - this is the picot line. I think the picots make the pattern look very pretty, but they are purely optional.

fig 37
Pricking for Clover Leaf

27

THE BELLS

Istarted with one bell design, but trying to decide which filling should be used soon convinced me that I should offer you more than one! 'Six of the best' has a nice ring about it, then I decided to ring the changes by making Carrickmacross and Needlelace bells as well - this made my 'peel' a complete scale of eight!

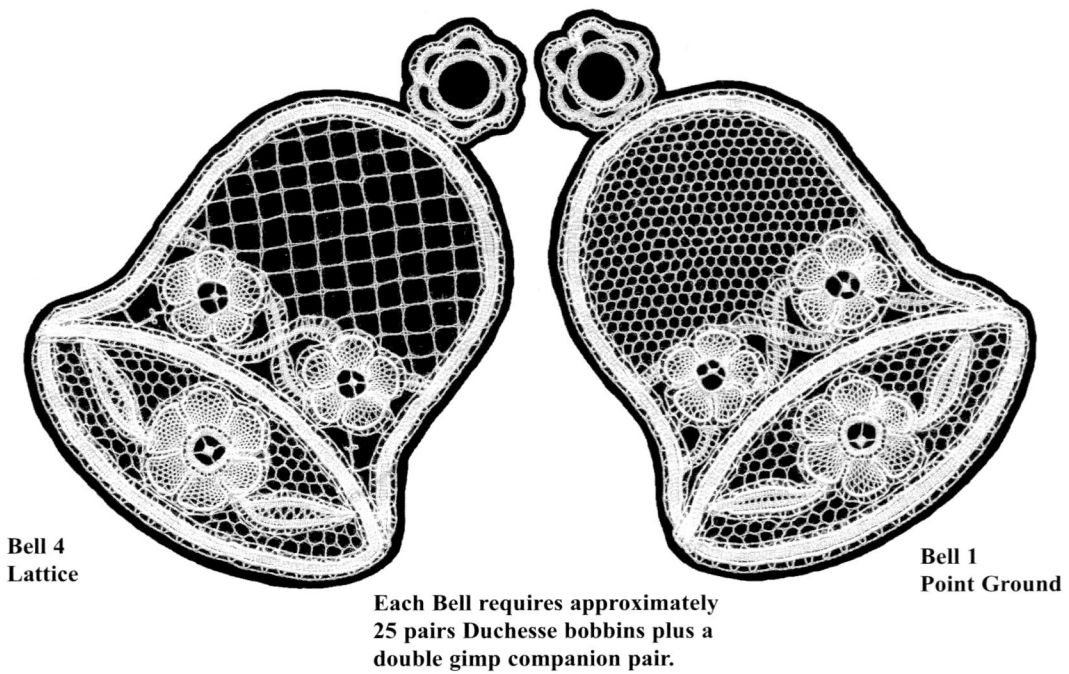

Bell 4
Lattice

Bell 1
Point Ground

Each Bell requires approximately 25 pairs Duchesse bobbins plus a double gimp companion pair.

Work a straight edge start at **A** *(fig 38)* with 6 pairs and a double gimp companion pair.

Make the edge; work the gimp pair through in whole stitch, giving you a gimp pair on either side of the braid.

Work the braid in whole stitch until you reach **B**, adding in an extra pair to give you 9 pairs in total (including the double gimp companion pair). This is where you will make a turn; leave your working pair here.

There are two ways a 'turn' may be worked: Method A takes the gimp companion pair across the braid to create a break; whereas Method B takes the inside gimp companion pair round the corner in it's original position.

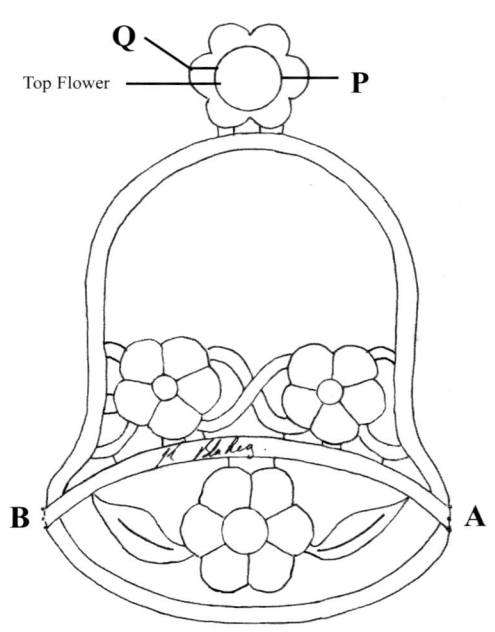

fig 38

The Bell working diagram may also be used as a pricking for your own filling and as a pattern for the Carrickmacross and Needlelace Bells.

28

Method A *(fig 39)*

Work whole stitch unless otherwise specified.

Taking the passive pair next to the outside gimp companion pair as workers, work through the gimp companion pair to **C**; edge stitch and pin; work back through the gimp companion pair, 3 passive pairs and the other gimp companion pair; leave workers there (to later become passives).

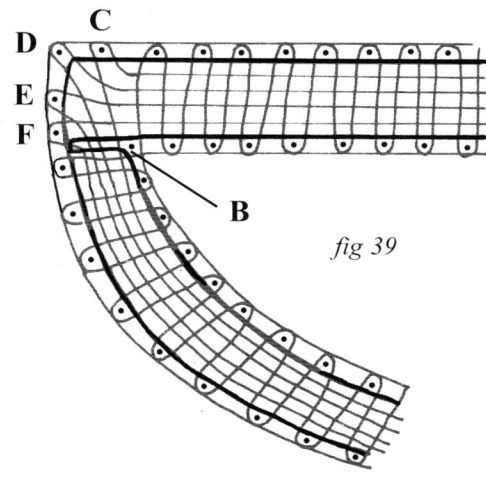

fig 39

Take the next passive pair as workers and work through the gimp companion pair to **D**; edge stitch and pin; work back through the gimp companion pair, 2 passive pairs and the other gimp companion pair; leave this pair next to the pair left from the previous row.

With the third passive pair, work through the gimp companion pair to **E**; edge stitch and pin; work back through the gimp companion pair, 1 passive pair and the other gimp companion pair; leave this pair next to the pair left from the previous row.

Taking the fourth passive pair, work through the gimp companion pair to **F**; edge stitch and pin; work back

Whole stitch and twist with the 2 gimp companion pairs that are now next to each other.

Take the RH pair of the gimp companion pairs and work in whole stitch back to **B** through the 4 passive pairs.

With the original worker pair left at **B** and the edge pair, make an edge stitch, pin; continue working the braid in whole stitch.

through the gimp companion pair; leave this pair here.

Method B *(fig 40)*

Work in whole stitch throughout.

Taking the passive pair next to the outside gimp companion pair as workers, work through the gimp companion pair to **W**, edge stitch and pin; whole stitch back through the gimp companion pair and the 3 passive pairs; leave workers next to the inside gimp companion pair (to later become passives).

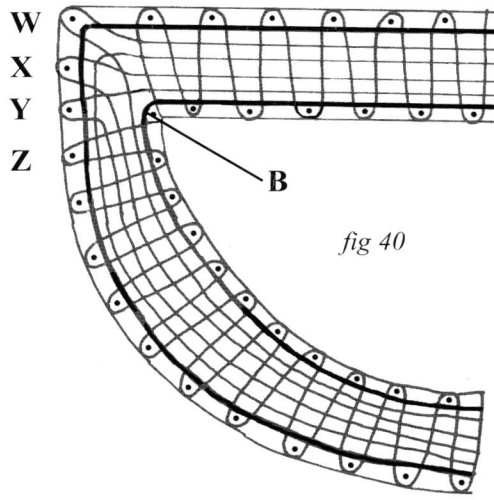

fig 40

With the 3rd passive pair, work through the 2nd passive and gimp companion pair to **X,** edge stitch, pin; work back through the gimp companion pair and 2 passive pairs; leave.

Take the 4th passive pair and work through the 2nd passive pair and the gimp companion pair to **Y**, edge stitch, pin; work back through the gimp companion pair and 1 passive pair; leave.

With the original working pair and the edge pair at **B**, make an edge stitch and pin; whole stitch through the inside gimp companion pair, 4 passive pairs and the outside gimp companion pair; edge stitch and pin at **Z**.

Finishing both Methods

Upon reaching the start at **A**, join here, then work over the top of the braid; attach at the other side; continue in whole stitch right round the Bell until you reach **B** again, sew in here using a Brugge Tie.

LARGE FLOWER

Using a straight start at the centre of the flower, rib round the centre with 6 pairs and join at the start; transfer pairs to the petal and add a gimp companion pair.

The flower is worked in half stitch and the petals are divided by the gimp.

Complete the flower with a small tally.

Continue working braid in whole stitch.

SMALL BELL FLOWER

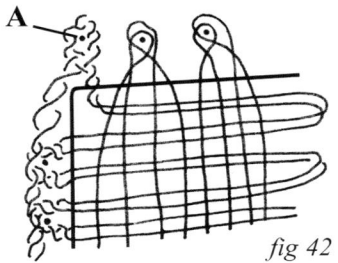

fig 42

Place 5 pins evenly spaced in the centre circle of the flower *(fig 41)*; take a piece of thread and wind it round the pins six times; tie it off. Place 3 pins along the edge of the petal and hang 6 pairs open *(fig 42)*.

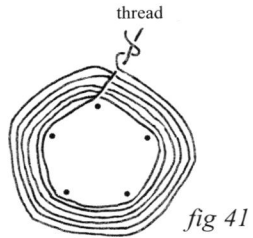

fig 41

With the pairs on pin **A**: twist each pair twice; whole stitch and two twists; add a gimp companion pair.

Work the flower in half stitch, using the ring of the thread in the centre for sewings; the centre is completed with a small tally.

LEAF

Hang 4 pairs on the braid and place the double gimp companion pair on a support pin.

Work the leaf in whole stitch adding 5 extra pairs (11 pairs including the double gimp companion pairs). A vein in the middle can be made either as a twist or a half stitch.

BAR

Sew 5 pairs in one of the small flowers and work the braid in whole stitch.

TOP FLOWER

With 6 pairs, using a straight start at **P**, rib round the centre; join at **P**; transfer pairs to make the petal.

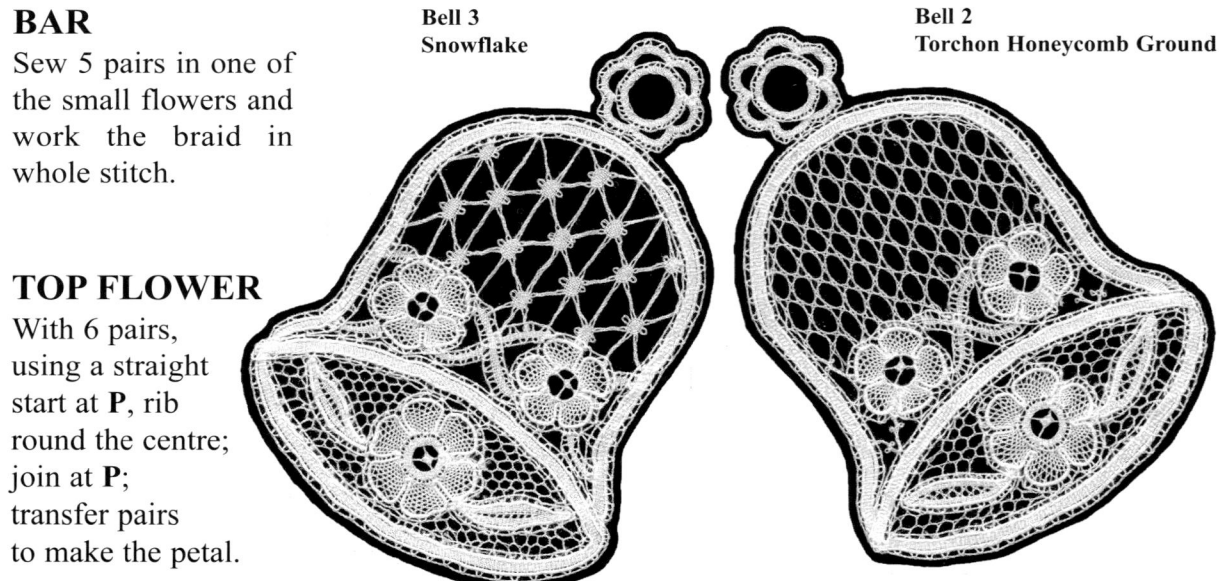

Bell 3
Snowflake

Bell 2
Torchon Honeycomb Ground

Rib round petal;

sew working pair into centre rib; work back through 2 passive pairs; leave workers there.

Take the last pair worked through and whole stitch to the centre, sew in; work in whole stitch to pin **Q**.

Take workers round the back of the pin; make an edge stitch; continue working the rib, repeating the joining at each petal section (as rib petal on *page 14*).

30

Bell 1
Point Ground

Bell 2
Torchon Honeycomb Ground

Bell 5
Whole Stitch Block

Bell 6
Bucks Honeycomb Ground

Bell 3
Snowflake Filling

Bell 4
Lattice Filling

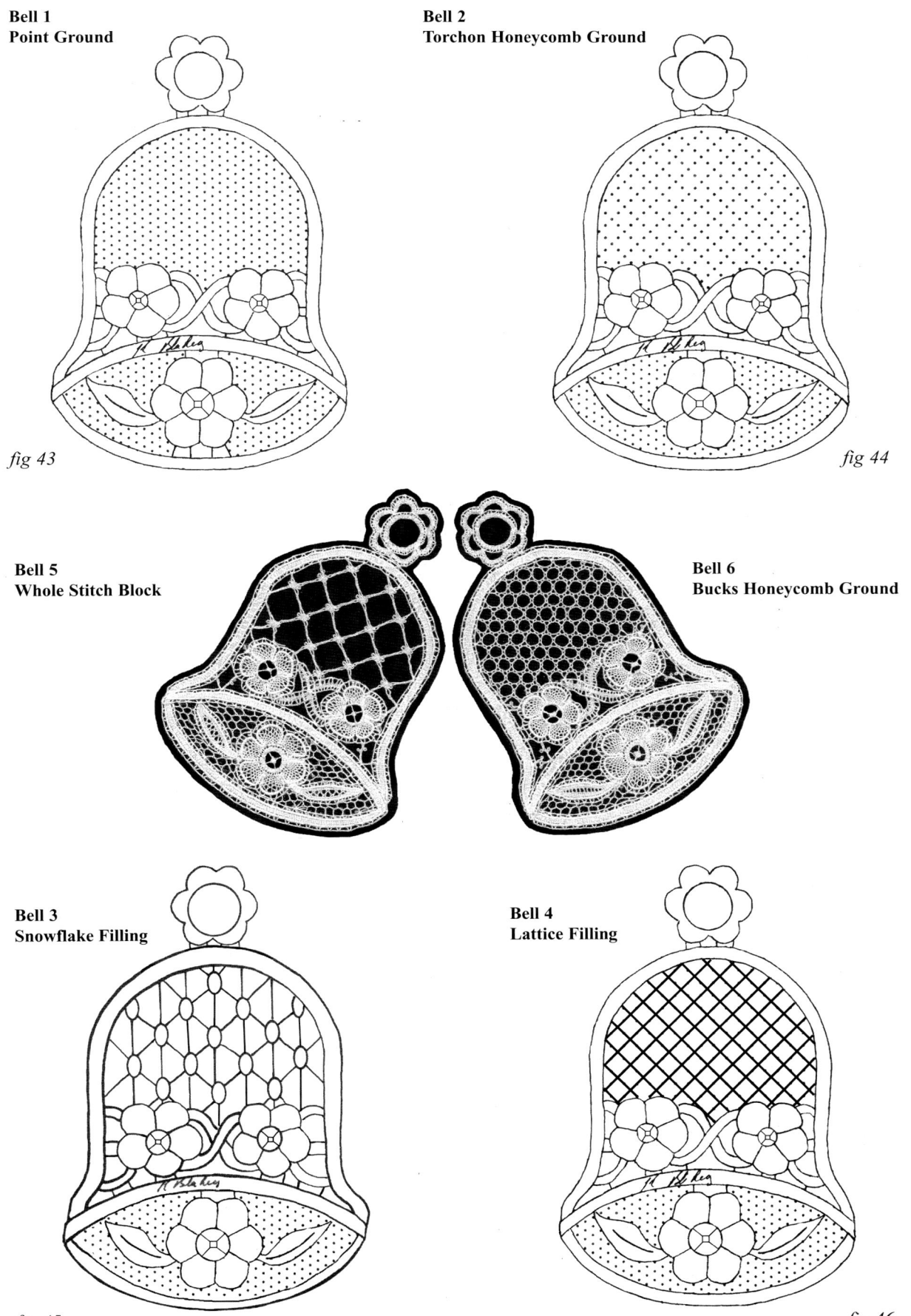

fig 43

fig 44

fig 45

fig 46

31

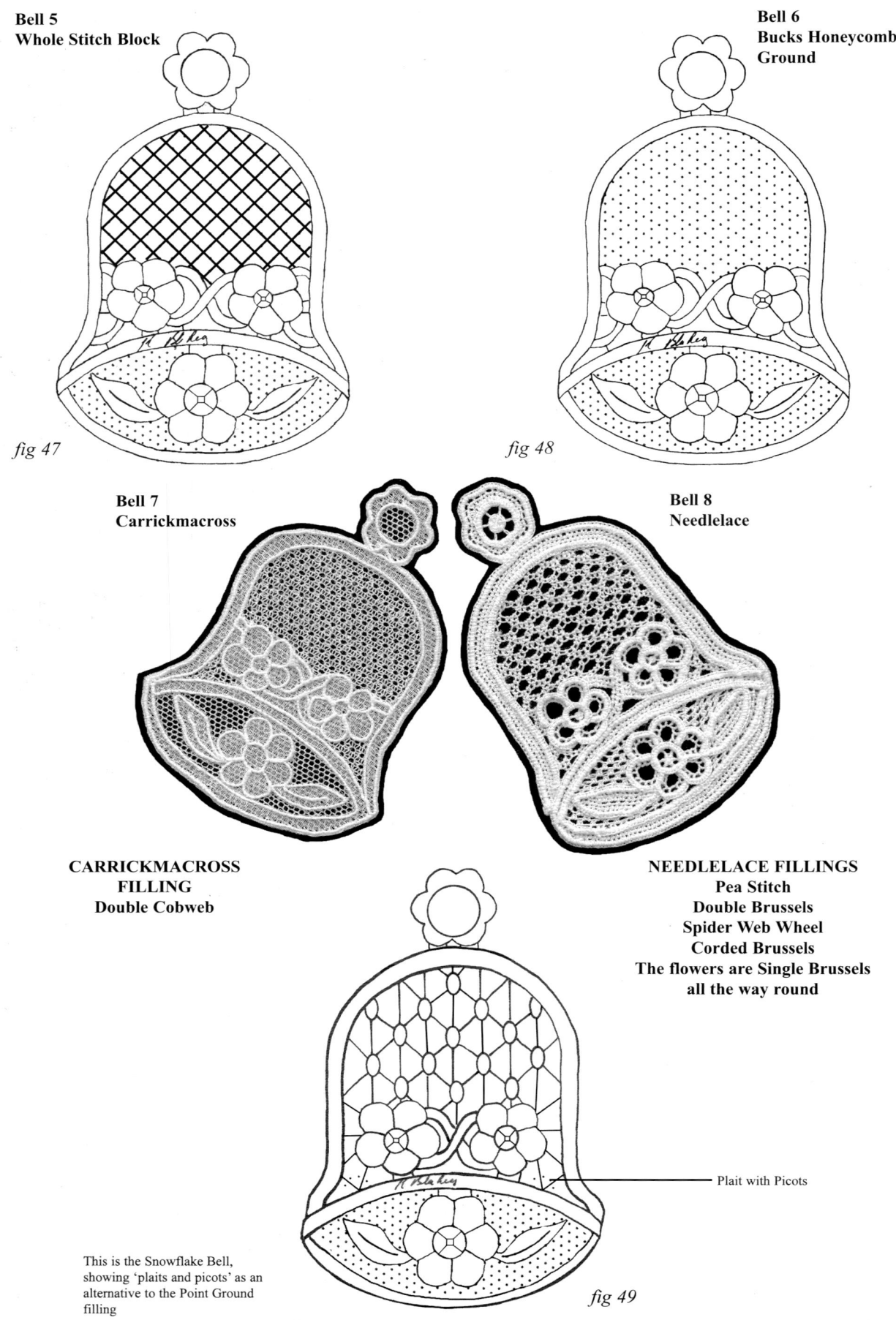

Bell 5
Whole Stitch Block

fig 47

Bell 6
Bucks Honeycomb
Ground

fig 48

Bell 7
Carrickmacross

Bell 8
Needlelace

CARRICKMACROSS
FILLING
Double Cobweb

NEEDLELACE FILLINGS
Pea Stitch
Double Brussels
Spider Web Wheel
Corded Brussels
The flowers are Single Brussels
all the way round

Plait with Picots

This is the Snowflake Bell,
showing 'plaits and picots' as an
alternative to the Point Ground
filling

fig 49

HONITON

DUCHESSE

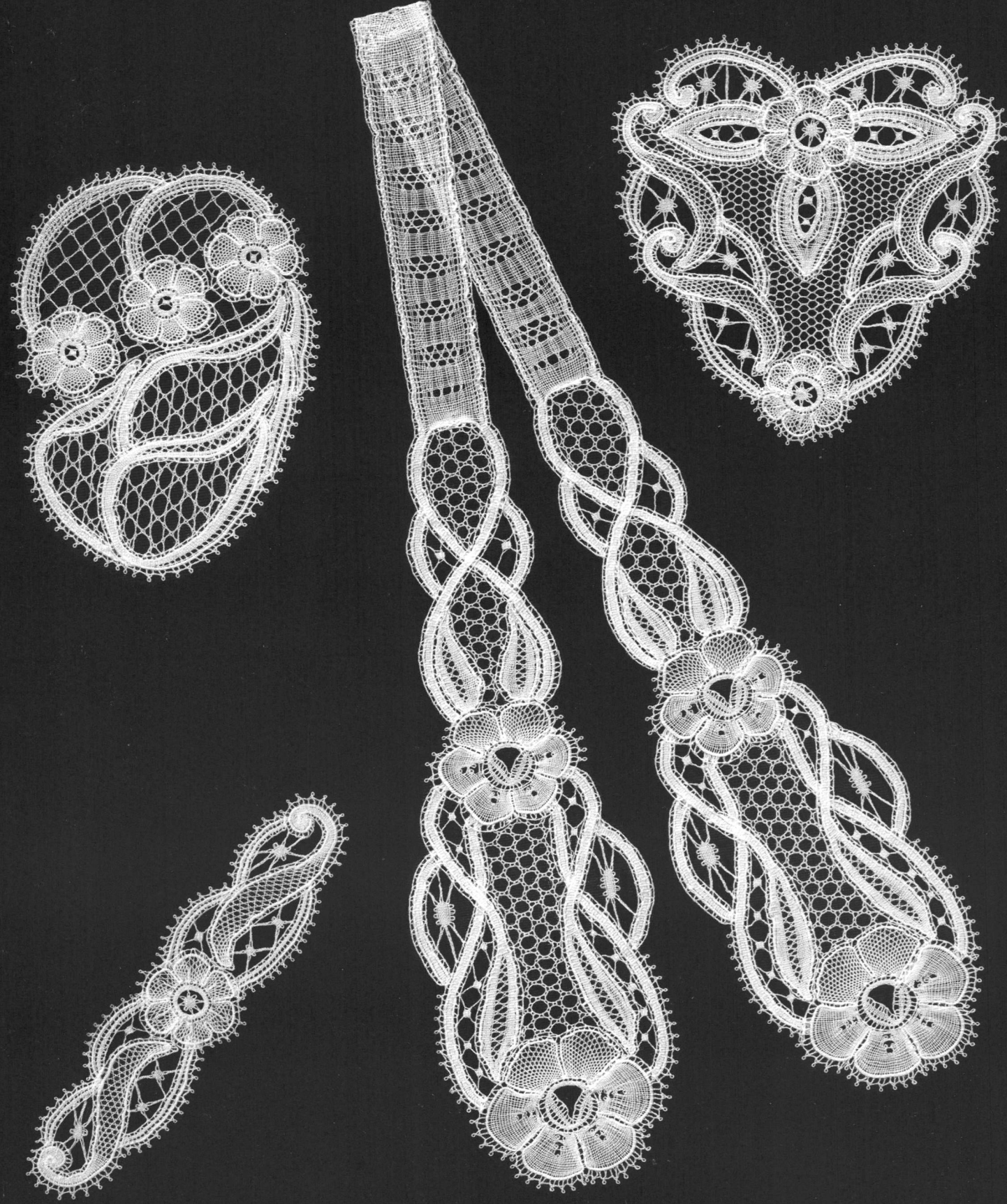

DUCHESSE

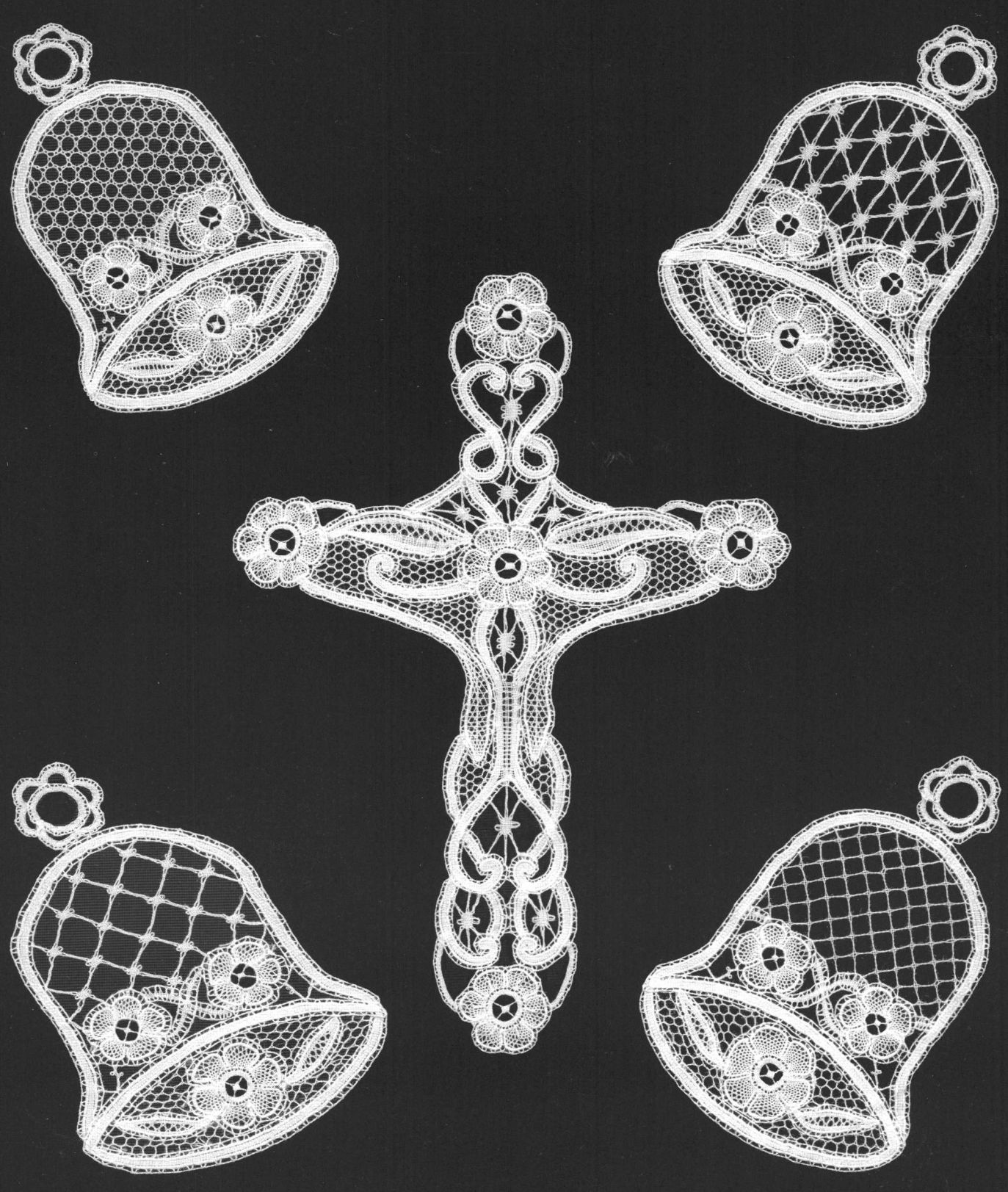

NEEDLELACE

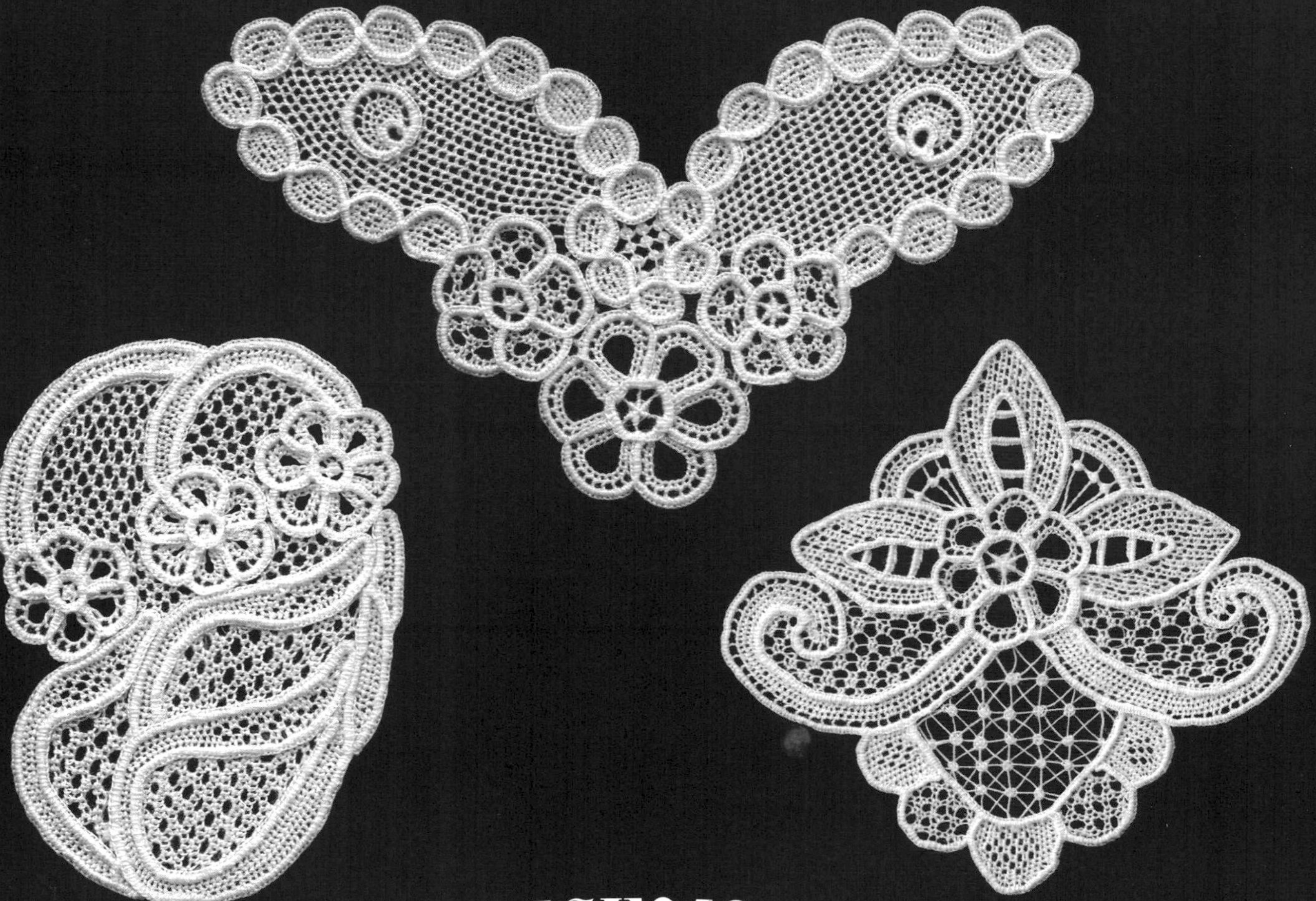

CARRICKMACROSS

TOGETHERNESS

 he idea for this design came to me when I was showing my young granddaughter how to draw circles!

DUCHESSE FILLINGS
Bucks Honeycomb Ground
Tallies

This pattern requires
approximately 24 pairs
Duchesse bobbins plus
1 gimp companion pair

FLOWERS

Make the 3 centre flowers first.
Each flower has a small rib in the
centre with half stitch petals and a
small tally filling.

CARRICKMACROSS FILLING
Diagonal Dot

LEAVES

The leaves are raised and rolled:
Starting with 6 pairs, rib up the centre of the
leaf; at the top add in 2 more pairs; work in
whole stitch back down the leaf.
As the work narrows take out pairs until 6
pairs remain; continue in whole stitch down
to the next join.
With 6 pairs roll *(see 'Duchesse Roll' page 11)*
up the side of the leaf just worked to the top
of the next section; then
work down again in whole
stitch; repeat this until
all sections are worked.
It is only in the large
section of the leaf that
2 extra pairs are needed;
all the other sections
are worked with 6 pairs.
Work each leaf the
same way.

CIRCLES

The outside of the circle is worked in whole stitch, with half stitch in the centre.

Starting at **A** *(fig 50)* with 5 pairs plus a gimp companion pair, work in whole stitch with a twist after the gimp pair on the outside edge; add in 3 extra pairs as it widens (9 pairs in total).

At **Z** start the half stitch centre; stop when you get to **B**.

At **C**, with 10 pairs and a scroll start, work the small section in whole stitch with a half stitch centre, until you reach **B**; then work altogether, gradually taking out the extra pairs until a total of 9 pairs remain.

Continue round the circle in this way working each small section as described, joining in the circle at **D** and **E**.

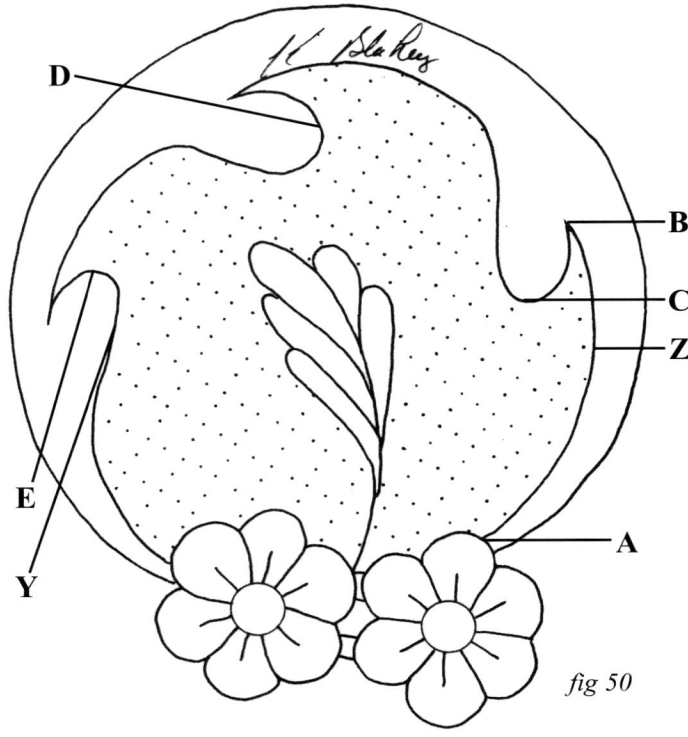

fig 50

Change back to whole stitch when you reach **Y**; decrease down to 5 pairs plus the gimp pair. Sew into the flower; bundle across to the next circle and start again.

When all three circles are completed, work the honeycomb filling. A picot edge may be worked if desired - the sample was done without.

fig 51

Both this pricking and the working diagram *(fig 50)* may also be used as a patterns for Carrickmacross and Needlelace.

MERRY GO ROUND

I had no problem designing this pattern for the top of a box, but putting a name to it was a different matter - I have just about worn a hole in the paper with the number of names that have been put in and rubbed out, but I think my final choice describes my feelings perfectly!

DUCHESSE FILLINGS
Inside: Bucks Honeycomb Ground
Outside: Point Ground
Snowflake

The picots on the outside edge are optional.

Merry Go Round requires approximately 20 pairs Duchesse bobbins plus a double gimp companion pair.

LARGE FLOWER

With 6 pairs make a rib round the centre of the flower *(fig 52)*; join at the point it was started and work the pairs across to be used in the petal.

Add a further 5 pairs and the gimp companion pair.

All the petals are worked in whole stitch: with one of the top pairs, work through all the pairs down to the rib; sew in at the joining hole then work back to the edge, edge stitch, pin; work back again to the next hole.

Sew into the rib; work the next 2 pairs (these pairs will be left to make a small plait). Continue to the edge, edge stitch, pin; work back to the pinhole in the 'V' *(fig 52a)*, twist, pin; leave out pairs here for a plait.

Work back to the edge, edge stitch, pin; work to the next pinhole; leave out only 1 pair here.

Work back to the edge, edge stitch, pin; work to the point of the 'V'; twist the single pair left out three times.

Make a small plait with each of the 2 pairs left out.

Take the pairs back in when working their respective pinholes.

Whole stitch to the end of the petal and make the normal division.

Work each petal the same way.

Sew in the pairs at the end; finish off with a Brugge Tie.

Work the snowflake filling.

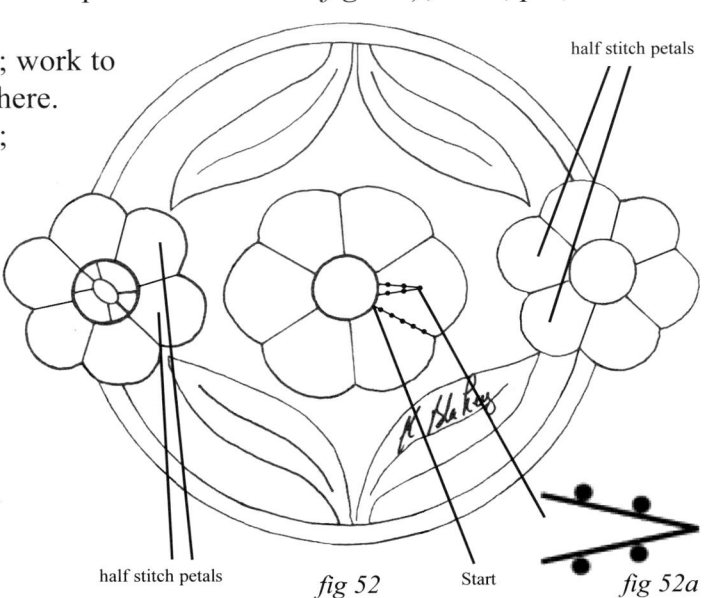

half stitch petals

half stitch petals

fig 52   Start   *fig 52a*

35

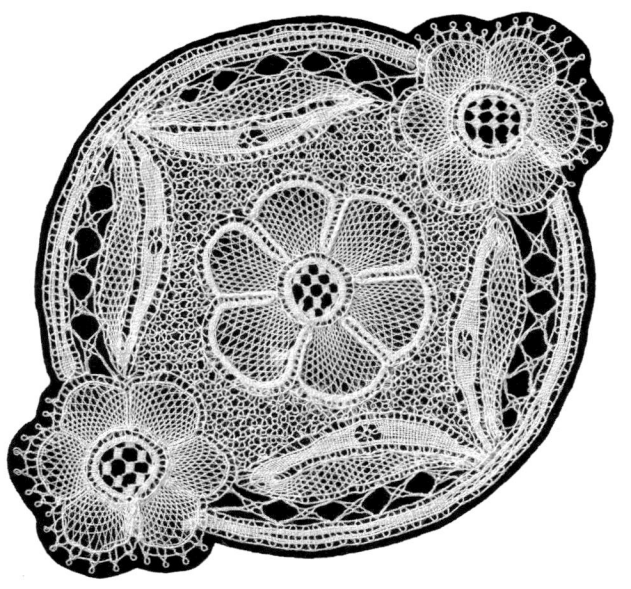

HONITON FILLINGS
No Pin (Swing Leadworks)
Four Pin
Half Stitch Plaits
Ebberley Grid

SMALL FLOWER

Starting with a 6 pair rib in the centre, the flower is worked using the same basic method as the small flower in 'Pearl Butterfly' *(page 19)*. However, work 2 of the petals half stitch, and make a snowflake in the centre of the flower.

The Merry Go Round pricking may be used for Duchesse and Honiton and as a pattern for Needlelace and Carrickmacross.

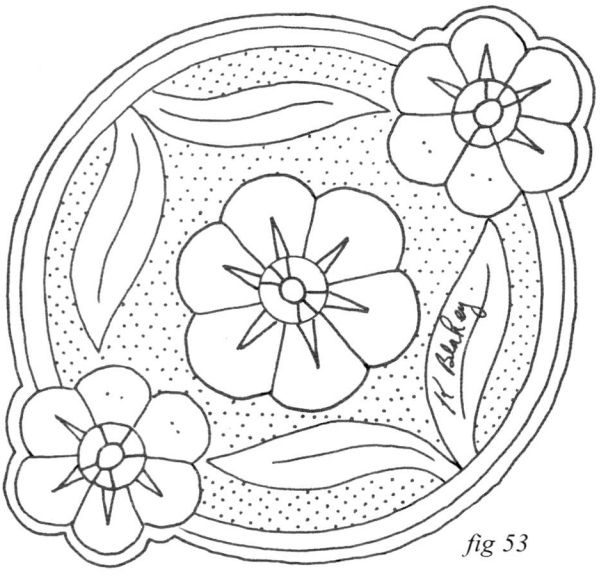

fig 53

LEAF

Point start with 6 pairs and a double gimp companion pair; increase to 14 pairs with a single half stitch passive pair down the centre to make a vein.

All four leaves are worked in the same way: whole stitch with one half stitch in the centre.

CARRICKMACROSS FILLING
Triple Dot

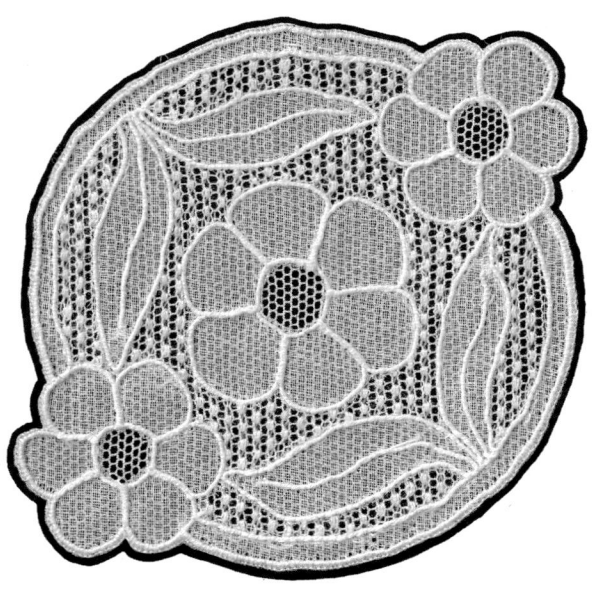

OUTSIDE BARS

Sew 6 pairs into one of the flowers and put the 2 gimp companion pairs on a support pin. Work the bar in whole stitch with a twist after the gimps on the outside edge.

Continue until the bar is completed. Sew into the next flower; tie off with a Brugge Tie.

FLORAL DANCE

The flowers represent children dancing round in the playground, skirts flared out and holding hands.

DUCHESSE FILLINGS
Point Ground
Tallies

This pattern requires approximately 24 pairs Duchesse bobbins plus 1 gimp companion pair.

fig 54

The working diagram may also be used as a pattern for Carrickmacross and Needlelace

Using 5 pairs, start the rib in one of the centre flowers at **Z**; rib round the centre of the flower, then close. Transfer the 5 pairs to the petal, adding in a gimp companion pair (6 pairs in total); with these pairs work the petals in half stitch. Complete the flower by making a small tally in the centre.

Each flower is worked the same way.

starting point **Z**

37

fig 55

Pricking for Duchesse
version of Floral Dance.

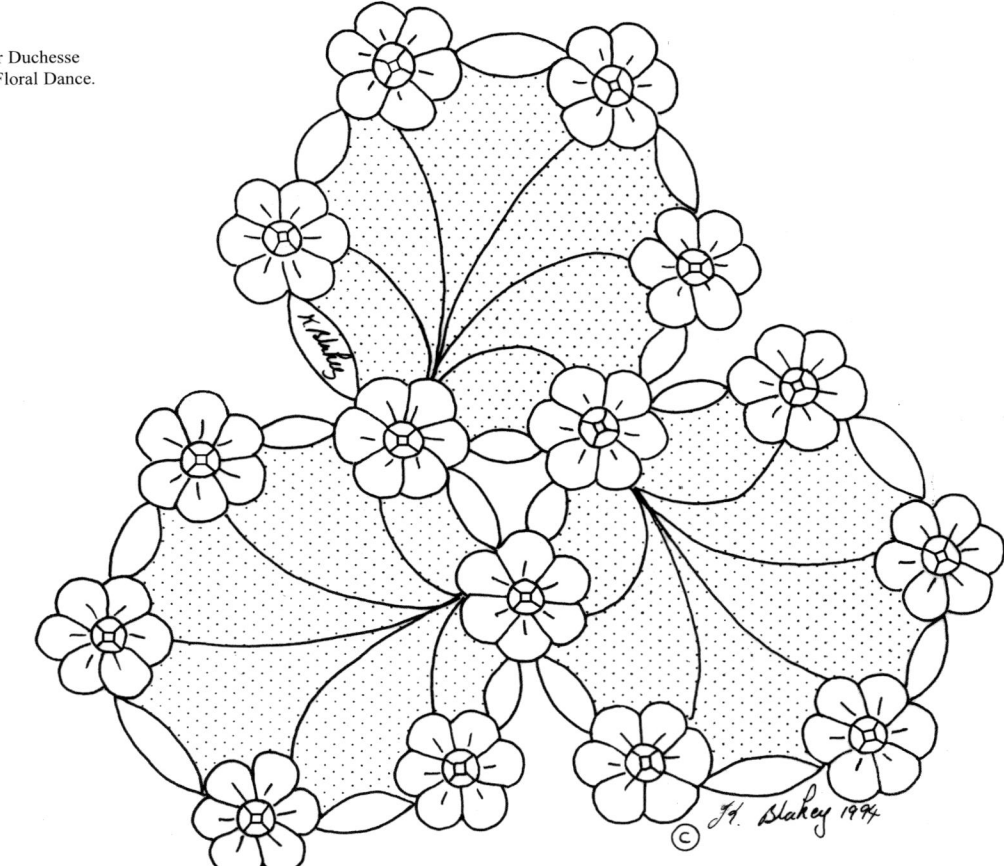

**CARRICKMACROSS
FILLINGS**
Double Cobweb
Diagonal Dot

The small leaves are worked in whole stitch, with a twist on the worker pair down the centre.

Each leaf is started with 5 pairs plus a double gimp companion pair; increase to a total of 9 pairs, including the double gimp companion pair.

The stems between the flowers are worked in a 6 pair rib. Start with the centre rib at **A** *(fig 54)*, then the 2 small ribs at **B** and finishing with the two medium ribs at **C**.

On completing each circle, work the point ground filling over the top of the ribs, making occasional sewings where necessary to hold the rib in place. By working each circle in turn, a large amount of filling is not left to work at the end.

There are three small tallies in the centre of the three circles.

CROSS

I have been asked many times for a cross pattern - here you see the result. I found it an interesting pattern to design as I did not want the cross to be too heavy or too light. I hope you feel as I do that this appears to be about right.

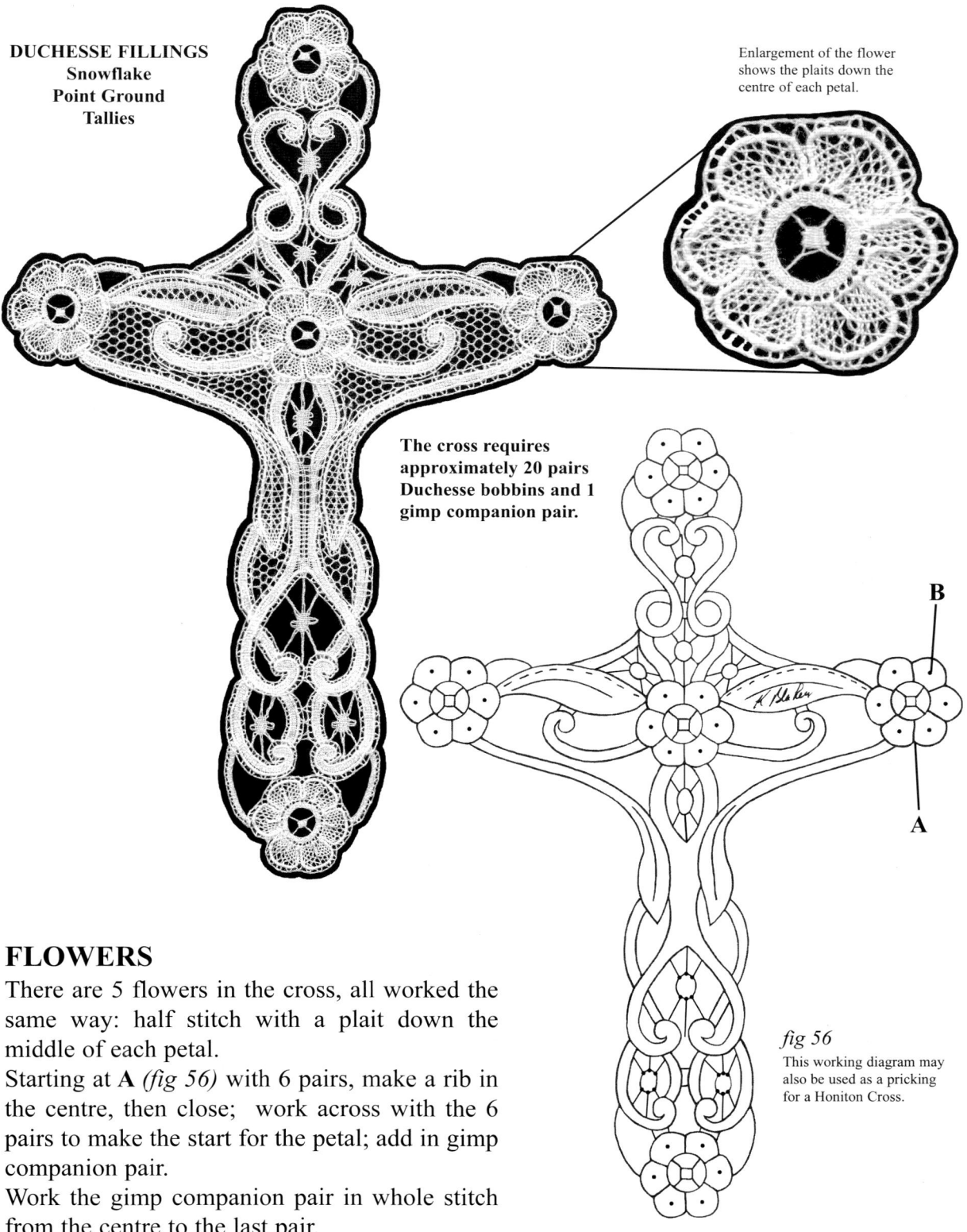

DUCHESSE FILLINGS
Snowflake
Point Ground
Tallies

Enlargement of the flower shows the plaits down the centre of each petal.

The cross requires approximately 20 pairs Duchesse bobbins and 1 gimp companion pair.

B

A

fig 56
This working diagram may also be used as a pricking for a Honiton Cross.

FLOWERS

There are 5 flowers in the cross, all worked the same way: half stitch with a plait down the middle of each petal.

Starting at **A** *(fig 56)* with 6 pairs, make a rib in the centre, then close; work across with the 6 pairs to make the start for the petal; add in gimp companion pair.

Work the gimp companion pair in whole stitch from the centre to the last pair.

Using the last pair worked through as workers, work back to the centre in half stitch.
Continue working the petal in half stitch; whole stitch through the gimp pair on the way out; half stitch on the way back through the gimps.
Work to the centre of the petal at **B**; whole stitch with the gimp; half stitch with the next 2 pairs; pin. These 2 pairs will now make the plait.
Lay the remaining pairs back and make the plait; sew it into the rib.
Put back into place the bobbins that were laid back; continue in half stitch.
Repeat this for each petal.
Finish with a tally in the centre.

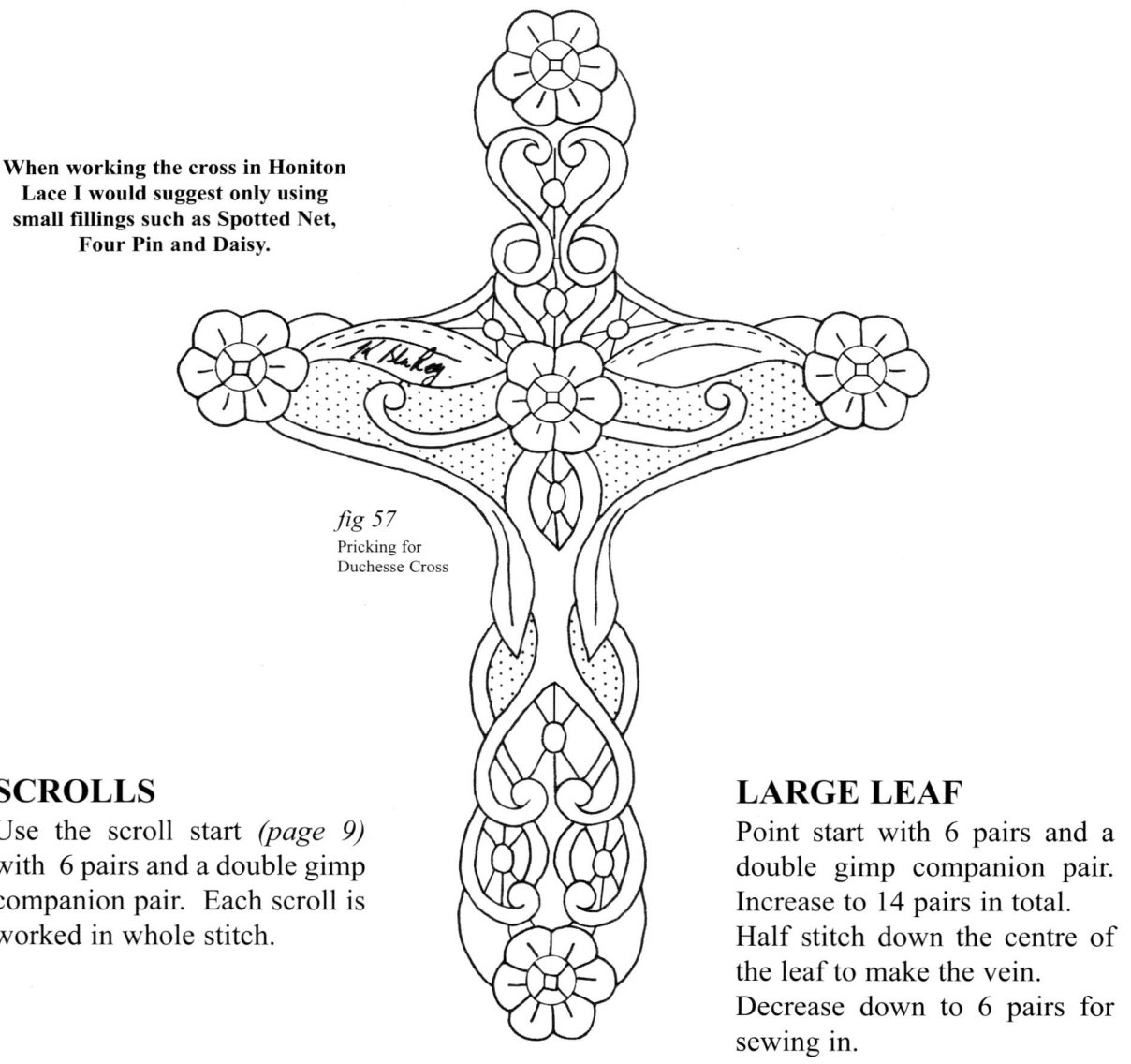

When working the cross in Honiton Lace I would suggest only using small fillings such as Spotted Net, Four Pin and Daisy.

fig 57
Pricking for
Duchesse Cross

SCROLLS

Use the scroll start *(page 9)* with 6 pairs and a double gimp companion pair. Each scroll is worked in whole stitch.

LARGE LEAF

Point start with 6 pairs and a double gimp companion pair. Increase to 14 pairs in total. Half stitch down the centre of the leaf to make the vein. Decrease down to 6 pairs for sewing in.

WILD ROSE

his pattern is a small neat edging for a handkerchief, designed for those of us who want to make an edging, but do not want to feel as if it is taking forever to complete.

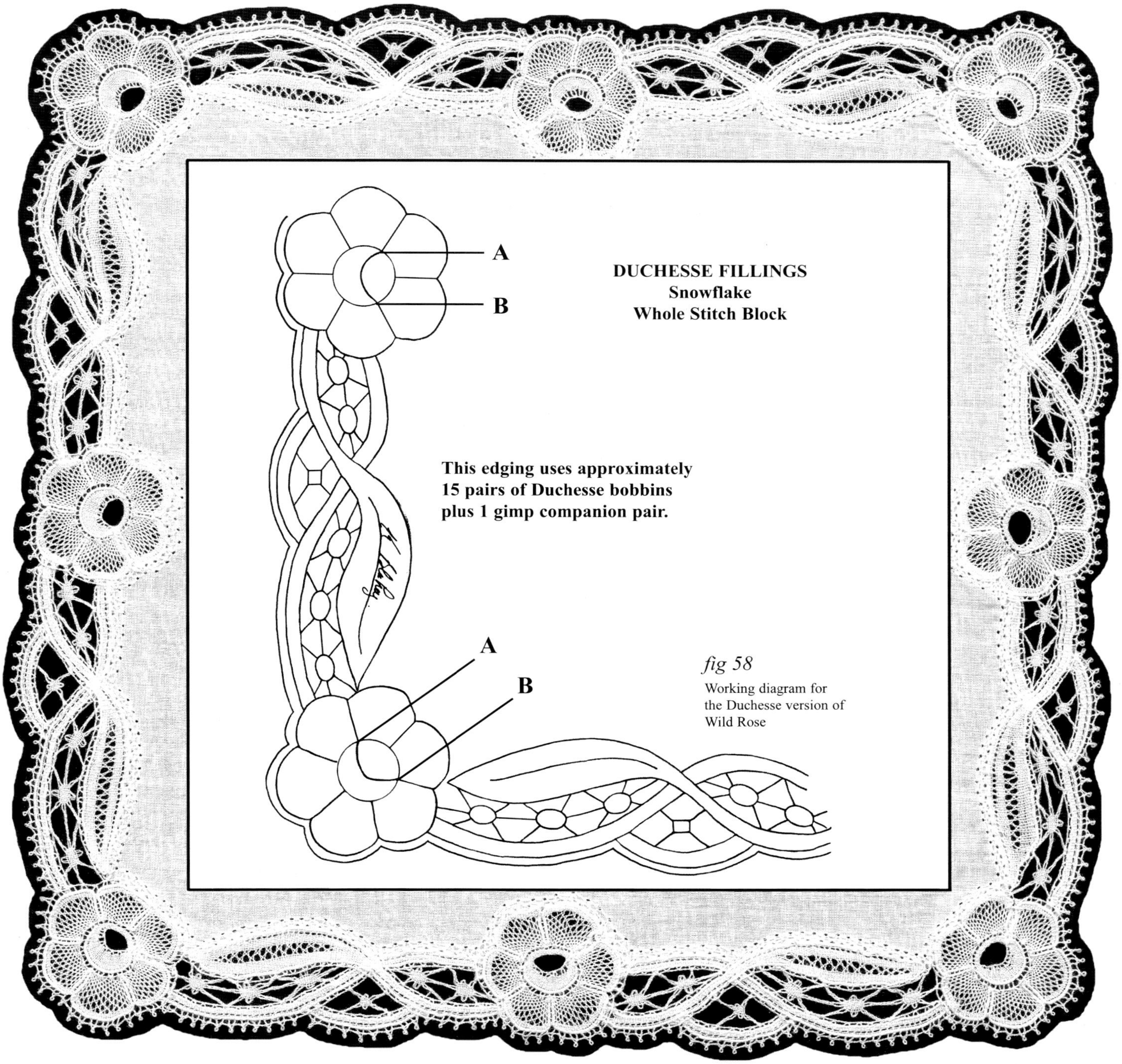

A

B

DUCHESSE FILLINGS
Snowflake
Whole Stitch Block

This edging uses approximately
15 pairs of Duchesse bobbins
plus 1 gimp companion pair.

A

B

fig 58
Working diagram for
the Duchesse version of
Wild Rose

41

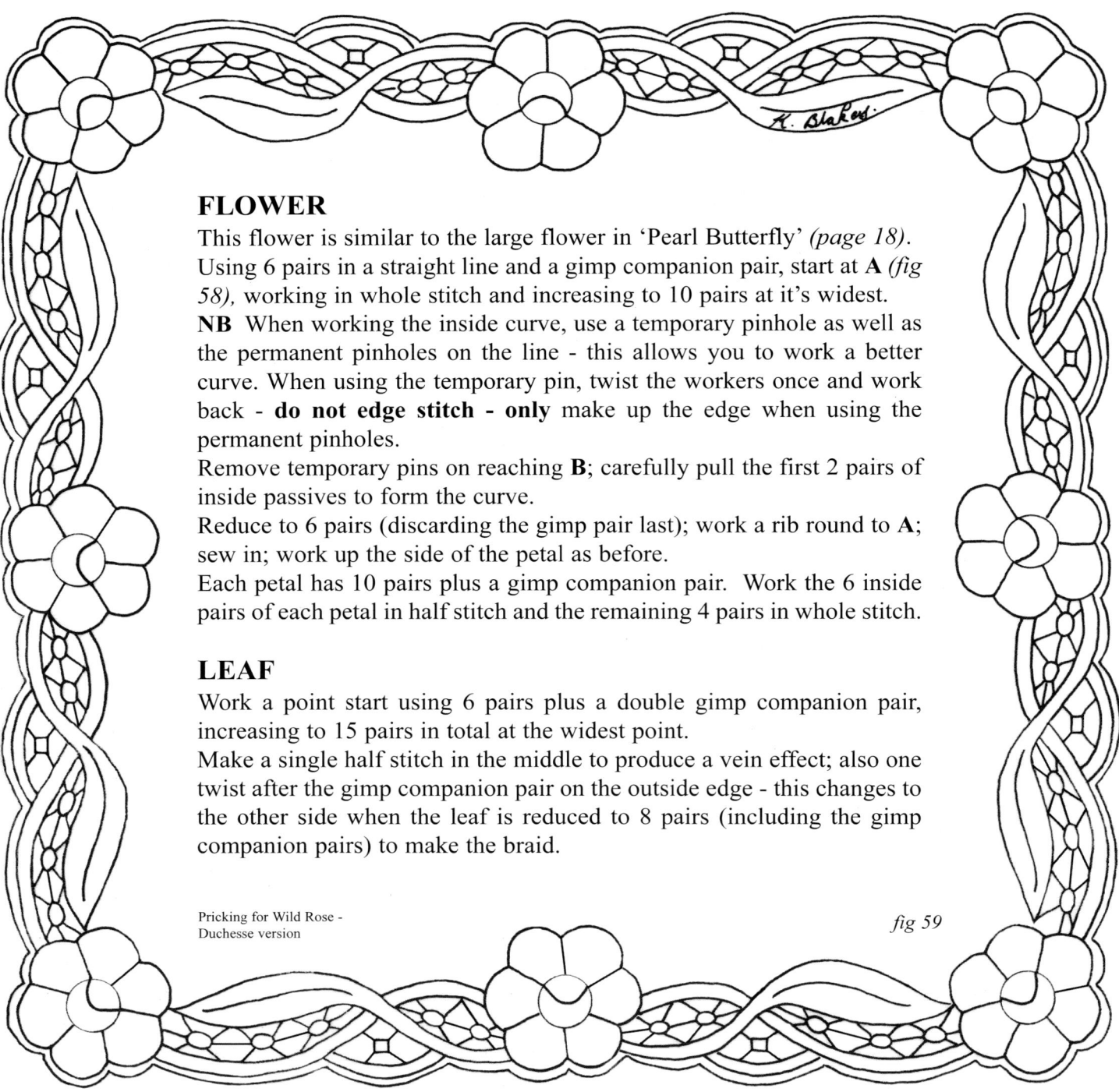

FLOWER

This flower is similar to the large flower in 'Pearl Butterfly' *(page 18)*.
Using 6 pairs in a straight line and a gimp companion pair, start at **A** *(fig 58)*, working in whole stitch and increasing to 10 pairs at it's widest.

NB When working the inside curve, use a temporary pinhole as well as the permanent pinholes on the line - this allows you to work a better curve. When using the temporary pin, twist the workers once and work back - **do not edge stitch - only** make up the edge when using the permanent pinholes.

Remove temporary pins on reaching **B**; carefully pull the first 2 pairs of inside passives to form the curve.

Reduce to 6 pairs (discarding the gimp pair last); work a rib round to **A**; sew in; work up the side of the petal as before.

Each petal has 10 pairs plus a gimp companion pair. Work the 6 inside pairs of each petal in half stitch and the remaining 4 pairs in whole stitch.

LEAF

Work a point start using 6 pairs plus a double gimp companion pair, increasing to 15 pairs in total at the widest point.

Make a single half stitch in the middle to produce a vein effect; also one twist after the gimp companion pair on the outside edge - this changes to the other side when the leaf is reduced to 8 pairs (including the gimp companion pairs) to make the braid.

Pricking for Wild Rose -
Duchesse version

fig 59

BRAID

Each braid is worked in whole stitch with 6 pairs plus the double gimp companion pair.
The outer edge of the braid has a twist after the gimp companion pair; the inner edge does not.

PICOTS

The flower and braids have picots on the outer edge, but they are purely optional.

FILLINGS

The fillings in this lace are Snowflake which requires 6 pairs of bobbins and Whole Stitch Block which requires 4 pairs of bobbins.

fig 60

The pricking for the Honiton corner and
this working diagram for the whole
edging may also be used for
Carrickmacross and Needlelace.

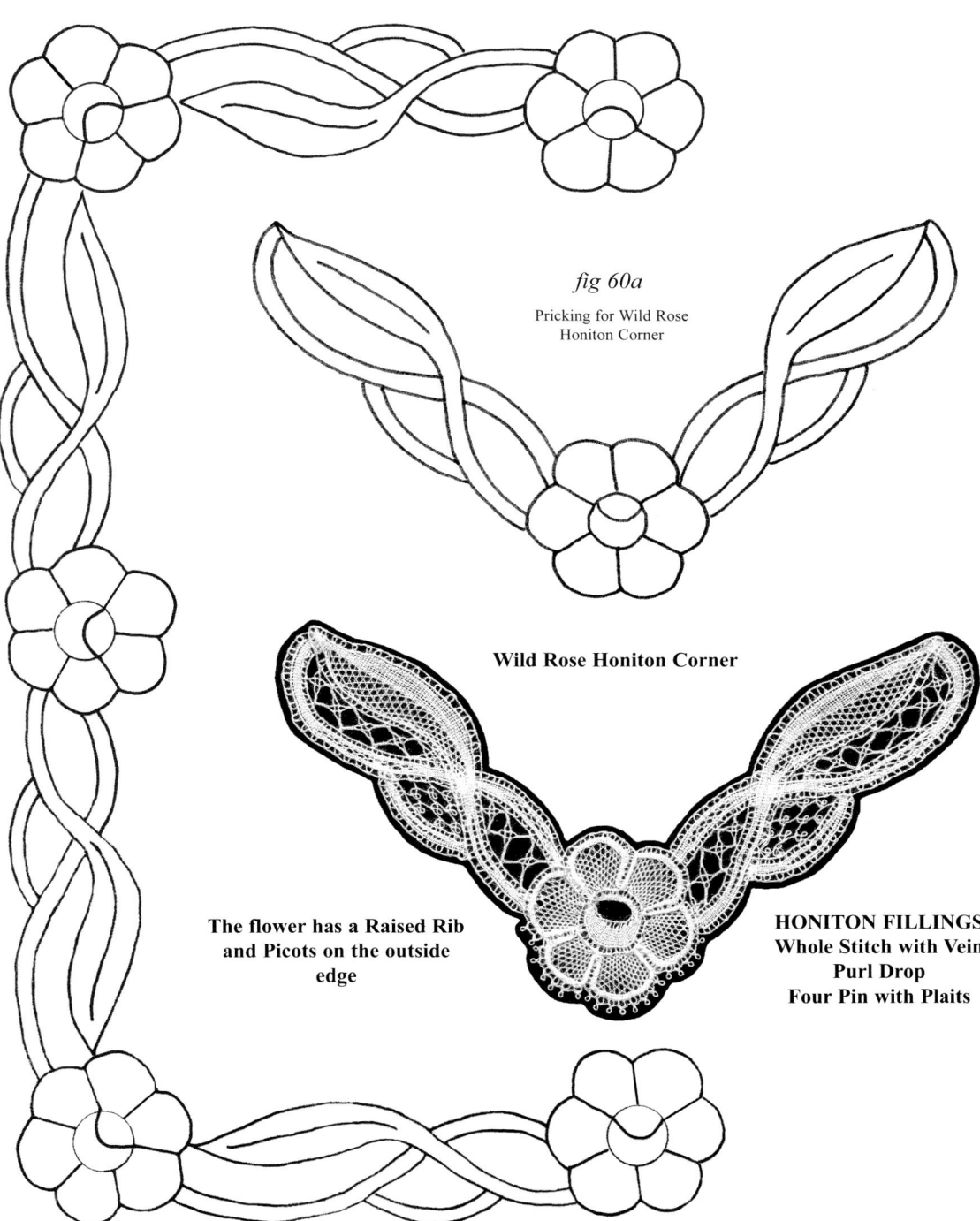

fig 60a

Pricking for Wild Rose
Honiton Corner

Wild Rose Honiton Corner

**The flower has a Raised Rib
and Picots on the outside
edge**

**HONITON FILLINGS
Whole Stitch with Vein
Purl Drop
Four Pin with Plaits**

SEA SPRAY

*S*ea Spray is another one of my 'phone call doodles', done whilst chatting to a friend who was as usual discussing a lace problem.

DUCHESSE FILLINGS
Lattice
Torchon Honeycomb Ground
Tallies

The filling in the Bars is
Lattice [tw x 3, wh st, tw x 3
with each pair]; the filling for
the Leaves is an Oval
Honeycomb.

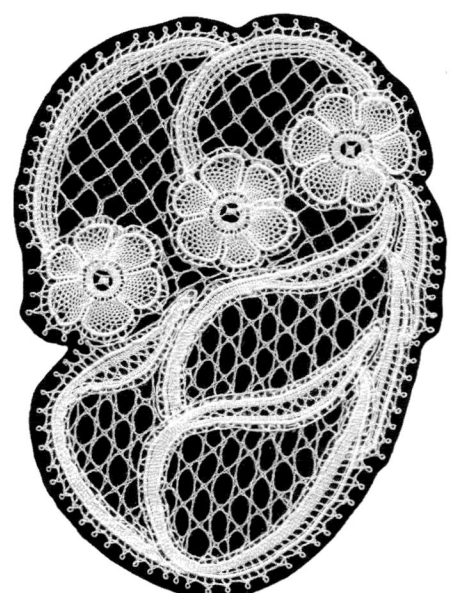

You will need 25 pairs
Duchesse bobbins plus
one gimp companion pair

FLOWERS

All three flowers are worked the same way. Using 5 pairs, make the rib in the centre and close; take these pairs across to start the petals of the flower adding in 2 pairs plus a gimp companion pair; work in half stitch.

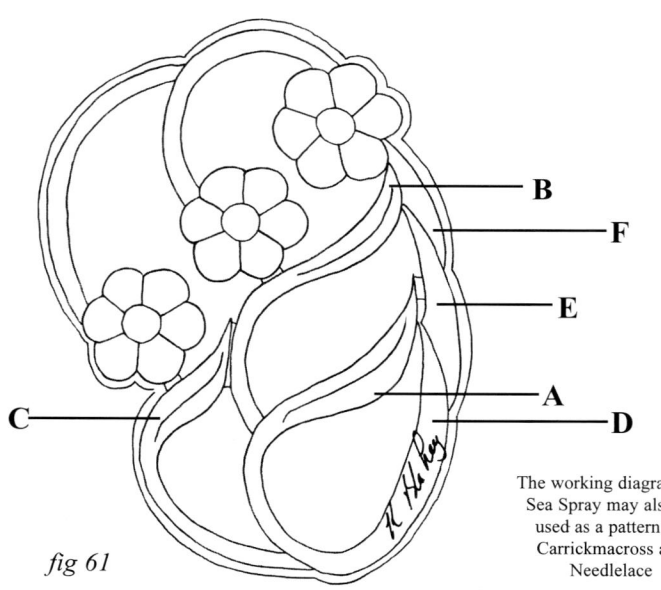

fig 61

The working diagram for
Sea Spray may also be
used as a pattern for
Carrickmacross and
Needlelace

BARS

Work the bars with 6 pairs plus a gimp companion pair for the outside edge. The bars are worked in whole stitch with a twist; a whole stitch and twist in the centre and a picot on the outside edge.

LEAVES

The leaves are worked in the order **A, B, C** *(fig 61)*. For leaf **A**, start at the point with 6 pairs plus a double gimp companion pair.

Work in whole stitch with a half stitch centre as the leaf widens; change back to whole stitch as the leaf narrows for the braid; add in extra pairs as the braid again widens into leaf **D**.

Leaf **D** is worked in whole stitch with a twist after the gimp companion pair on the outside edge.

Leaves **B** and **C** are worked in whole stitch with a half stitch centre.

The small half leaves **E** and **F** are worked in whole stitch with a twist after the gimp companion pair on the outside edge.

NEEDLELACE FILLINGS
Pea Stitch
Double Brussels
Corded Brussels with alternate Holes
Single Brussels
Spider Web Wheel

fig 62
Pricking for Duchesse version of Sea Spray - may also be used for Honiton, Carrickmacross and Needlelace

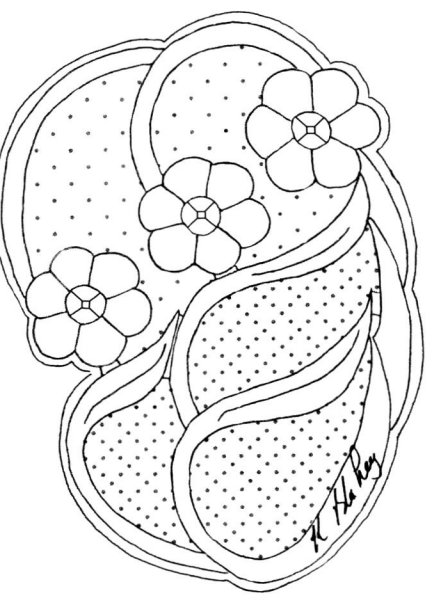

CARRICKMACROSS FILLINGS
Triple Dot
Diamond

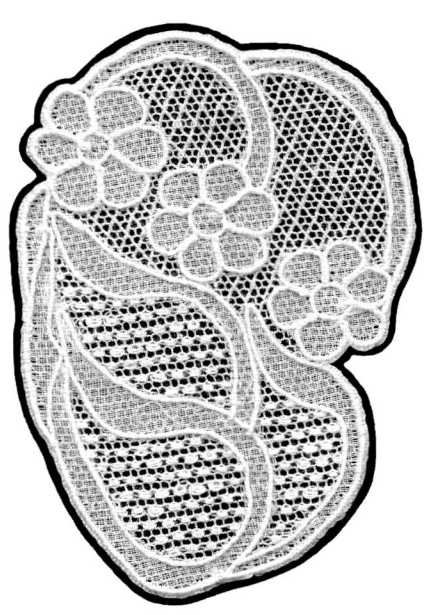

There is a picot edge all round the design, but the design may be worked without the picots, if you wish, by omitting the outside line.

45

ELLA

This design is dedicated to a dear friend who died suddenly. Ella liked the design at first sight and declared that she would be the first to make it up. Sadly, she passed on before the details were completed.

FLOWER

Start at the flower in one of the corners.

Using 6 pairs, work a rib in the centre of the flower starting and closing at **A** *(fig 63)*.

Take the pairs from the rib and a gimp companion pair across to start the petals of the flower in half stitch; complete the flower with 4 small tallies.

LEAVES

Use 6 pairs to start the leaf at **B** with a rib round the outside edge; join at the flower; bundle across to the inside edge *(see page 12)* and rib round the inside edge; close at the flower.

Use 4 pairs from the rib to work the half stitch leaf filling; spread out evenly using 3 passive and one worker pair. I found this was quite enough to fill the space.

Finish each leaf with 2 tallies.

DUCHESSE FILLINGS
Snowflake
Tallies
Lattice
Whole Stitch Block

To work this design you will need
16 - 20 pairs Duchesse bobbins
plus 1 gimp companion pair.

snowflake

B

A

E

C

latttice

D

whole
stitch
block

picot
edge

BARS

Complete all 3 leaves, then work the bars **C** [whole stitch with a twist] in the middle of the bar, using 6 pairs plus a gimp companion pair; fill the space with a snowflake.

Start at the flower in one of the corners.

Using 6 pairs, work a rib in the centre of the flower starting and closing at **A**.

NEEDLELACE FILLINGS
Corded Brussels with Holes
Corded Brussels
Pea Stitch
Pea Stitch (second variation)
Point D'Angleterre Wheel Filling No 2
Spider Web Wheel
Wheel Ground No 1 (variation)

fig 63

SCROLLS

Use a Scroll Start at **D**, work the scrolls in whole stitch with a half stitch down the centre. Finish off by sewing in at the flower.

CORNER

Sew in at **E** with 6 pairs and make a rib round the inside edge; join at the scroll. Take the 6 pairs from the rib and work them across to start the petal, adding in 3 more pairs and a gimp companion pair. Work the petals alternately in whole stitch and half stitch, with a picot on the outside edge.

Complete all corners using the same method.

The side sections are all simple scrolls and bars with small tally fillings. The small flower is worked using the same method as the corner flower, but has only one tally in the centre.
The small lines between the sections are indications for the side sewings.

fig 64
Pricking for Ella

fig 65

This pattern for the Needlelace corner may also be used as a pricking for a Duchesse or Honiton corner.

48

ARABESQUE

DUCHESSE FILLINGS
Bucks Honeycomb Ground
Torchon Honeycomb Ground
Whole Stitch Block
Tallies
Plaits

**To complete Arabesque, you will need
approximately 20 pairs Duchesse
bobbins, 1 double gimp companion pair
and 1 gimp companion pair.**

49

Completely work each section before moving onto another.

Using 8 pairs and a double gimp companion pair, start with one of the heart shaped scrolls *(fig 66)*. Work in whole stitch adding extra pairs as necessary and work a decorative stitch of your choice.

Work each bar with 6 pairs and a gimp companion pair.

The heart is filled with Torchon Honeycomb Ground; the space next to the heart is filled with plaits; the larger space with whole stitch block.

fig 66

This working diagram would also be suitable for a Carrickmacross motif.

fig 67

Pricking for Honiton version of Arabesque

Each small circle is done in half stitch with 8 pairs plus a gimp companion pair.

The flower has a 6 pair rib in the centre; each petal is worked with 8 pairs plus a gimp companion pair.

Work the petal as follows: work the 3 pairs in the centre in whole stitch; the remainder in half stitch. Work each petal up one side and down the next. Bundle across the bottom, as described in Duchesse Techniques *(page 12)*, until all the petals are completed.
Four small tallies in the centre.
The centre is filled with Bucks Honeycomb Ground.

50

fig 68

Pricking for Arabesque.

The heart-shaped section would also be suitable as a
Duchesse or Needlelace Corner.

JABOT

I puzzled over the design for the Jabot a long time. Eventually I decided to make it in three separate pieces gathered at the top, instead of one long length. I designed three different Jabots, but this was the one chosen by most of my friends.

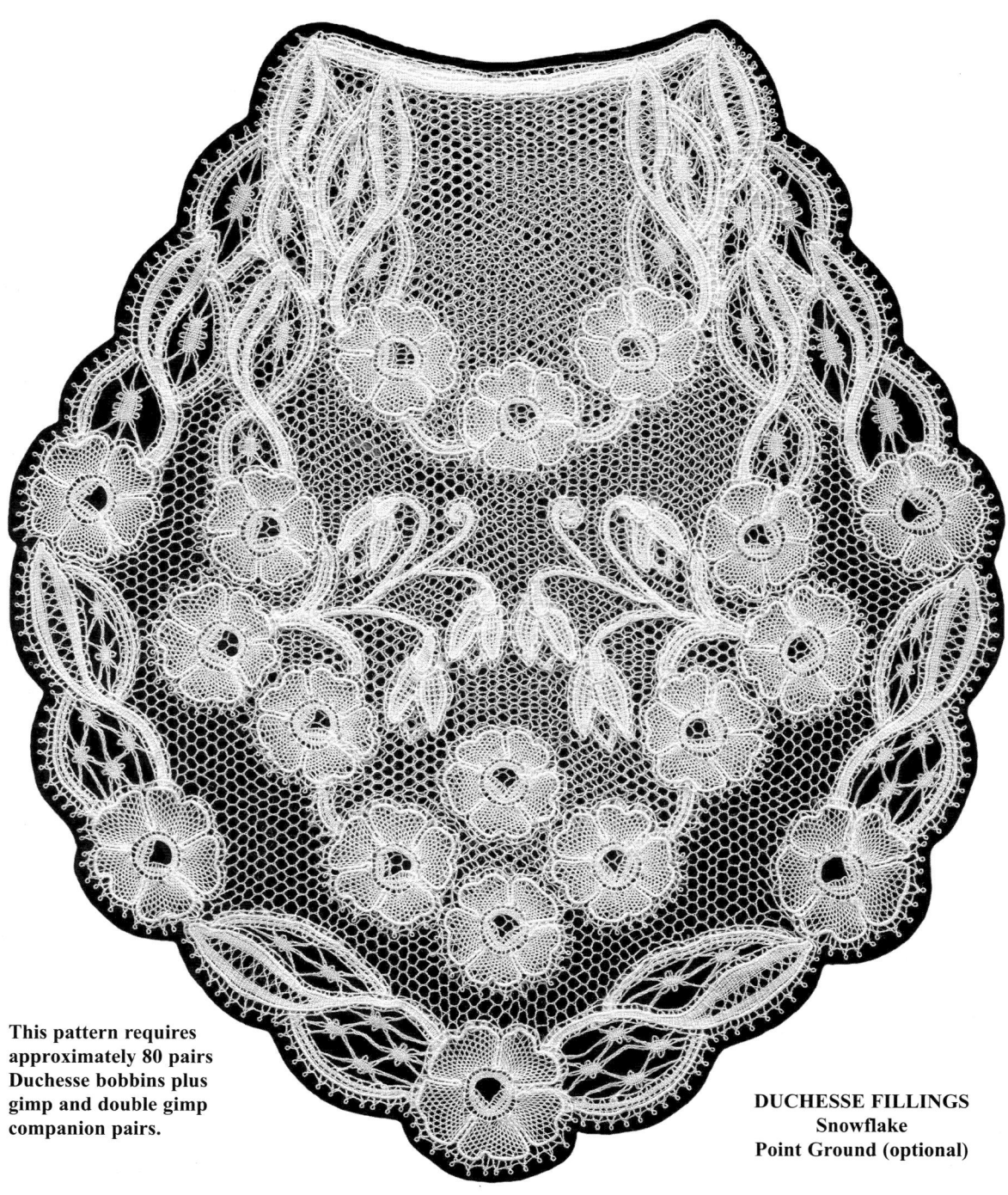

This pattern requires approximately 80 pairs Duchesse bobbins plus gimp and double gimp companion pairs.

DUCHESSE FILLINGS
Snowflake
Point Ground (optional)

I feel the middle section of the Jabot is the most intricate design, so I will describe the working of this section. The flowers, leaves and fillings are worked using the same method for all three sections of the Jabot.

FLOWER

Work the small petals in the centre of the flower first.

Using 7 pairs, make a point start; work in whole stitch with a twist in the middle of each petal. After the second petal has been worked, reduce to 6 pairs; continue in the rib to the start of the first petal; join here.

Transfer the pairs to the large petal, adding in 2 extra pairs and a gimp companion pair. Work all these petals in half stitch with a division made after each petal and picots on the outside edge.

LEAF

With 8 pairs and a double gimp companion pair, make either a point start or a join at one of the flowers. Work each leaf in whole stitch with a half stitch division down the middle, adding pairs as it widens.

The total number of pairs required is 14 including the double gimp companion pair. This is then reduced to 7 pairs including the gimp companion pair.

Continue in whole stitch **only** until the stem of the leaf is finished.

Make small picots on the outside edge of each leaf.

Work all the remaining leaves using the same method.

fig 69

Pricking for the middle section of the Jabot.

OUTSIDE BAR

Use 6 pairs and a gimp companion pair.

Work in whole stitch, with a twist after the gimp companion pair.

The gimp companion pair is laid in on the outside curved edge of the bar; a twist is made before you work it going out; a twist after you have worked it coming back.

INSIDE BAR

The inside bar is slightly smaller and requires only 5 pairs plus a gimp companion pair. Again, the gimp companion pair is laid in on the outside curved edge of the bar. The bar is worked in whole stitch.

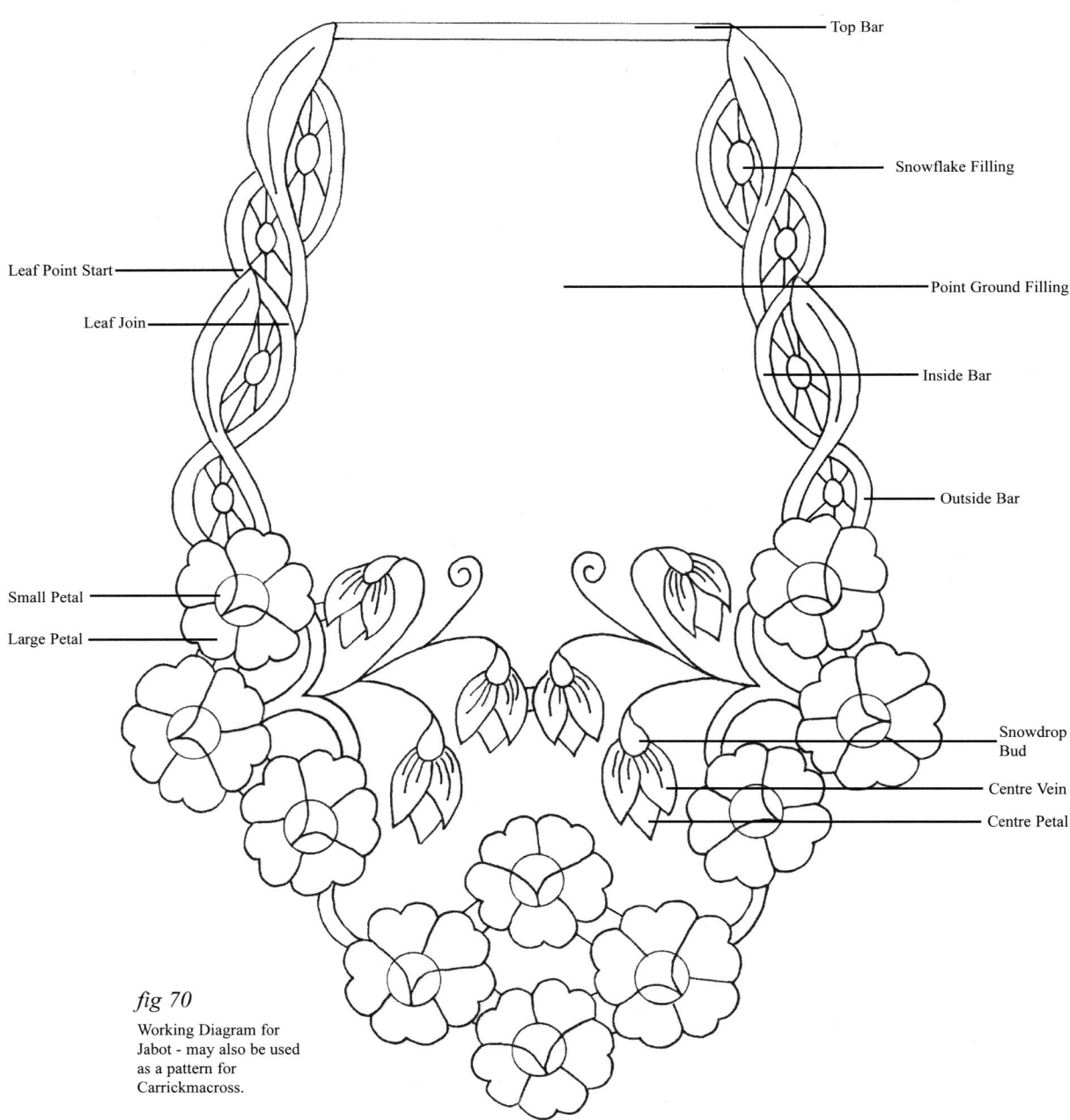

Top Bar

Snowflake Filling

Leaf Point Start

Point Ground Filling

Leaf Join

Inside Bar

Outside Bar

Small Petal

Large Petal

Snowdrop Bud

Centre Vein

Centre Petal

fig 70

Working Diagram for Jabot - may also be used as a pattern for Carrickmacross.

54

SNOWDROP BUD

With 6 pairs and a double gimp companion pair, work a curved start at the top of the bud. Work in whole stitch to the top of the stem; remove the double gimp companion pair. With the remaining 6 pairs work the stem in rib.

SNOWDROP PETAL

With 6 pairs and a double gimp companion pair, make a point start; work in whole stitch adding in 1 pair, to make 9 pairs in total.

There are three small vein lines made in each petal: start the centre vein first with one twist; repeat for a further two rows.

Bring the two remaining vein lines in, working the row as follows:

[edge stitch, 2 whole stitches, twist, whole stitch, twist, whole stitch, twist, 2 whole stitches, edge stitch].

Continue each row * to *, working down each petal to the bud; sew in.

The second petal is worked using the same method.

The centre petal is worked with 4 pairs as a small rib.

TOP BAR

Use 8 pairs and a double gimp companion pair; work in whole stitch.

The 8 pairs are sewn into the top leaf; the double gimp companion pair is held on a support pin and laid in.

FILLING

All the small spaces are either a small snowflake or a large snowflake.

The remainder is filled in with point ground, the number of bobbins varying from section to section - the largest section takes 80 pairs. It is advisable to have a whole day to do this filling!

NB If you do not wish to work the point ground filling, applique to a good quality cotton net.

MAKING UP

When all three pieces have been completed, they should be lightly sewn together on a drawing thread, pulled together to frill and then either attached to a ribbon to go under the collar of a blouse, or they can be attached by a brooch.

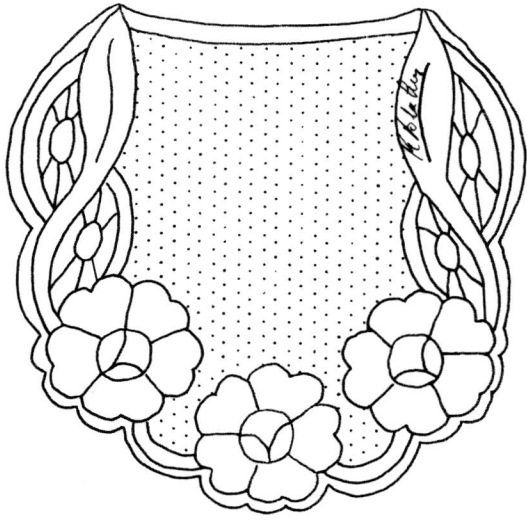

fig 71
Pricking for the top section of the Jabot - also suitable for Carrickmacross Lace.

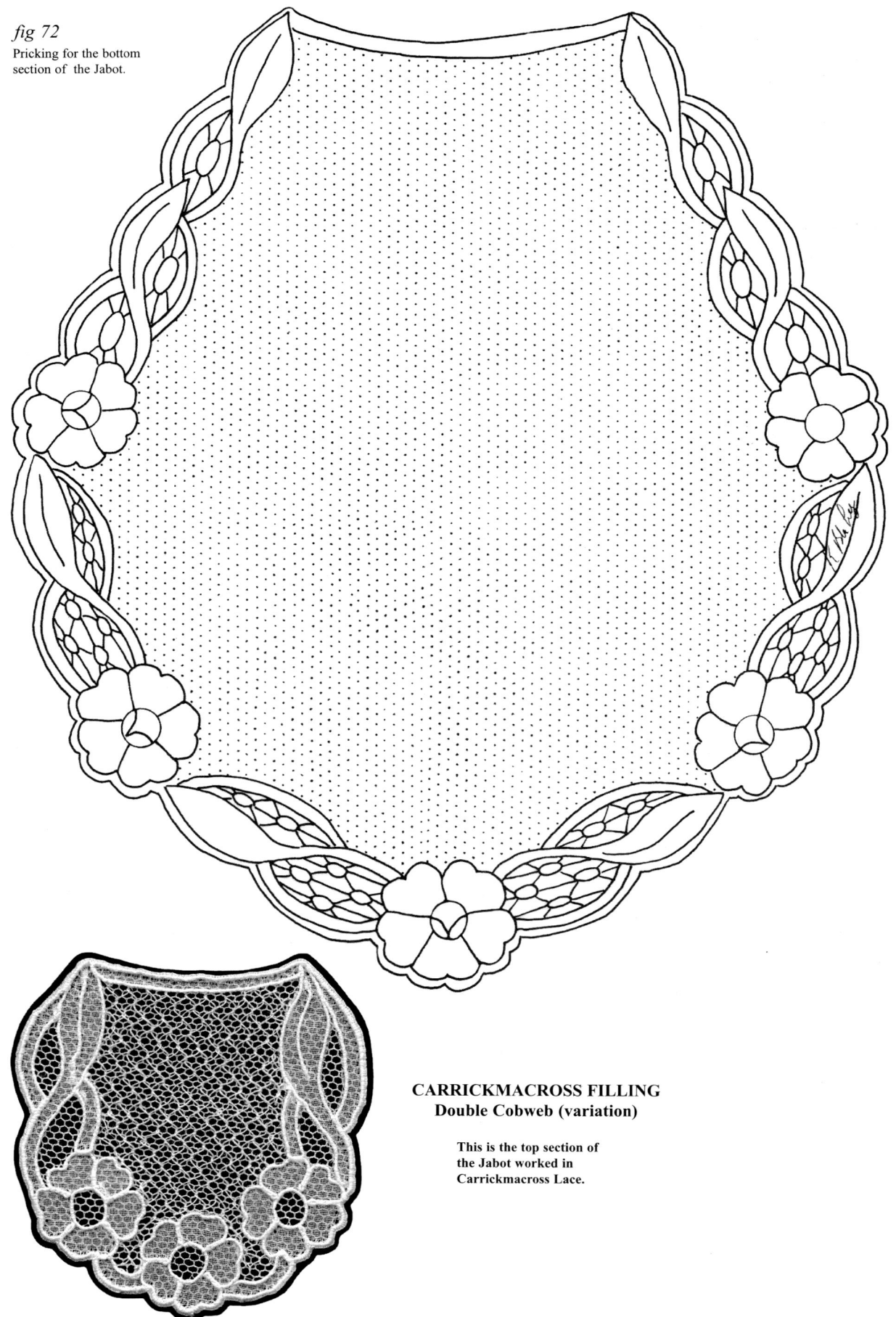

fig 72
Pricking for the bottom
section of the Jabot.

CARRICKMACROSS FILLING
Double Cobweb (variation)

This is the top section of
the Jabot worked in
Carrickmacross Lace.

FLORAL TIE

he Floral Tie was designed as an alternative to the Jabot, a simple accessory for the right occasion.

Each tie is worked separately - you will require approximately 20 pairs Duchesse bobbins plus gimp and double gimp companion pairs.

LARGE FLOWER

This flower is similar to the large flower in Merry-Go-Round *(page 35)*.

Starting at **A** *(fig 73),* with 6 pairs work in whole stitch, increasing to 7 pairs and making a small twist down the centre of the petal.

After completing the second small petal, reduce to 6 pairs; rib round the rest of the centre; join at the top of the first small petal.

Transfer the pairs from the centre to the first large petal; add 6 more pairs plus the gimp companion pair, (13 pairs altogether including the gimp companion pair).

Four petals are worked in whole stitch* and two in half stitch.

*The whole stitch petals have a small vein in the centre of each petal: work in whole stitch to the centre, sew in at the bottom of the vein; work back leaving out 2 pairs, edge stitch; work back to about a quarter of the way up the vein, pin, twist twice, leave out 1 pair, whole stitch back to the edge, edge stitch and a picot.

Whole stitch back to the top of the vein, pin, twist twice, work back to the edge.

With the pairs that were left out, make a small plait with each of the 2 pairs; the single pair is twisted twice.

Continue working the petal in whole stitch, taking in the original pairs that were left out at the correct pinholes.

Work all four petals in this way - change to half stitch for the last two petals.

DUCHESSE FILLINGS
Bucks Honeycomb Ground
Snowflake
Tallies

SMALL FLOWER

The small flower is worked the same way as the large flower, but with only 10 pairs including the gimp companion pair.

LEAF TRAIL

At the top of the leaf, sew 6 pairs into the large flower;
add in a double gimp companion pair, making 8 pairs in total; work in whole stitch increasing the pairs to 16.
A half stitch vein is worked down the centre of the leaf.
As the leaf narrows, gradually reduce the pairs to 8 (these are all that are required for the trail). Work the trail in whole stitch; sew out into the small flower.

BRAIDS

All the braids or trails are worked in whole stitch with 6 pairs plus a double gimp companion pair. Work all the braid trails before the small leaf is made.

SMALL LEAF

At the top of the leaf sew 8 pairs into the small flower; add in the double gimp companion pair; work in whole stitch with a half stitch vein in the centre, increasing the pairs to 14 (including the double gimp companion pair).
As the braid edge is used as the leaf edge, there is no edge stitch on the side next to the braid.

LARGE BRAID

A total of 21 pairs including the double gimp companion pairs are used in this braid.
The braid is worked in whole stitch and may be worked plain or decorative according to individual preferences.
The centre 12 pairs were used to make the pattern. A total of four inches of braid was worked on each section.

FINISHING OFF

A small piece of ribbon is joined to the braid ends - this can be adjusted for neck size.

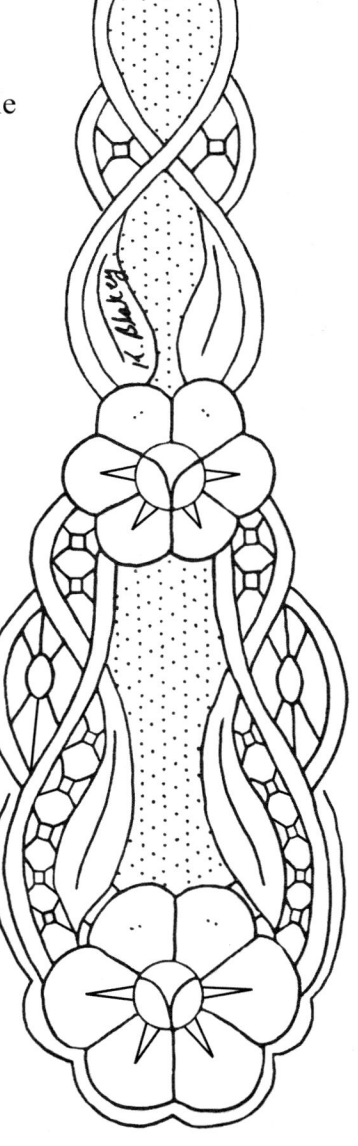

fig 73

Floral Tie pricking for Honiton, Carrickmacross and Needlelace.

fig 74

Pricking for Floral Tie in Duchesse Lace.

DOROTHY'S DELIGHT

This dressing table set caused great delight to my friend, Dorothy, as I was making it. She gave some helpful suggestions and some gentle teasing, both at the same time! It is a complete set comprising hair brush, hand mirror, clothes brush, powder bowl and tray.

CLOTHES BRUSH

DUCHESSE FILLINGS
(not all the fillings are used in each design)
Point Ground
Bucks Honeycomb Ground
Snowflake
Whole Stitch Block
Tallies

HAND MIRROR

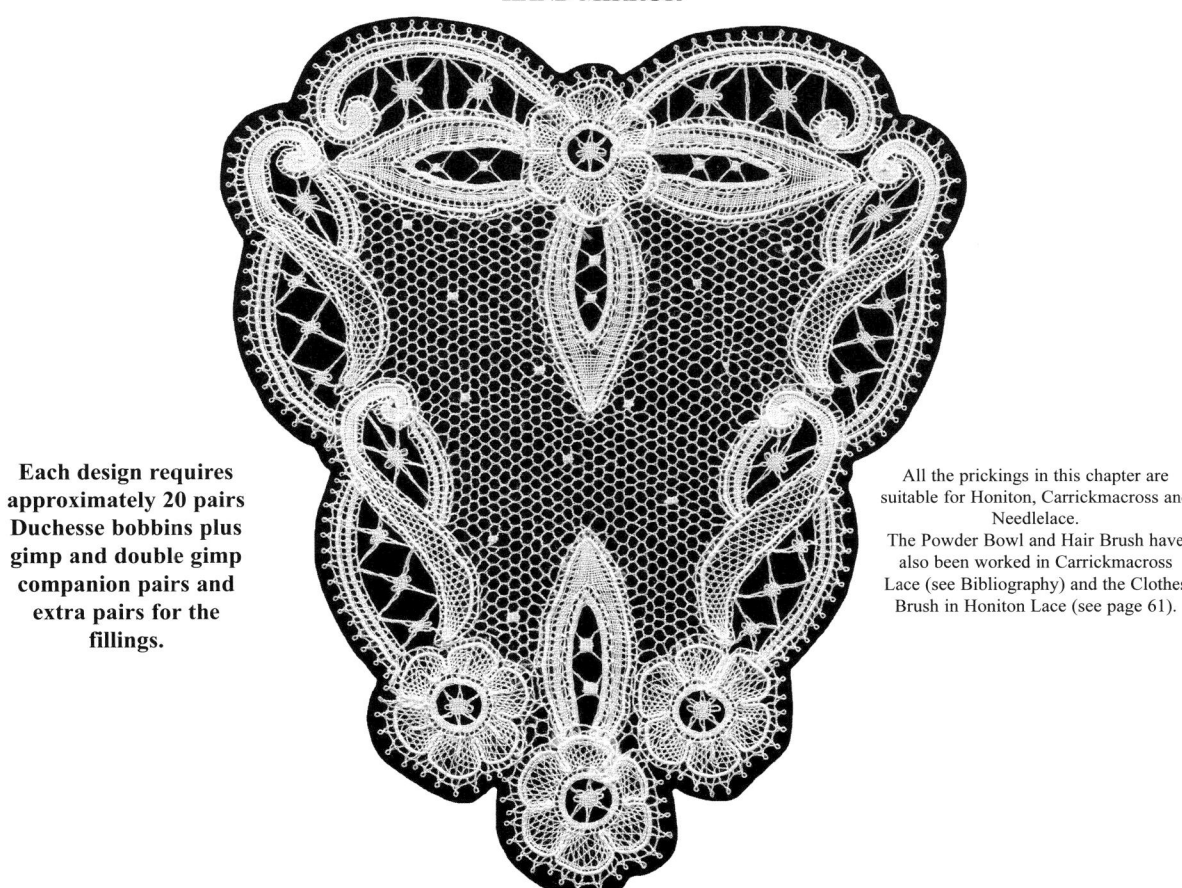

Each design requires approximately 20 pairs Duchesse bobbins plus gimp and double gimp companion pairs and extra pairs for the fillings.

All the prickings in this chapter are suitable for Honiton, Carrickmacross and Needlelace.
The Powder Bowl and Hair Brush have also been worked in Carrickmacross Lace (see Bibliography) and the Clothes Brush in Honiton Lace (see page 61).

I will describe the working of the tray (pictured on the back cover), which is the most intricate design in the set. The smaller designs are worked in the same way as the tray, with the exception of the net in the hand mirror design, where I have added a few small tallies as a variation.

59

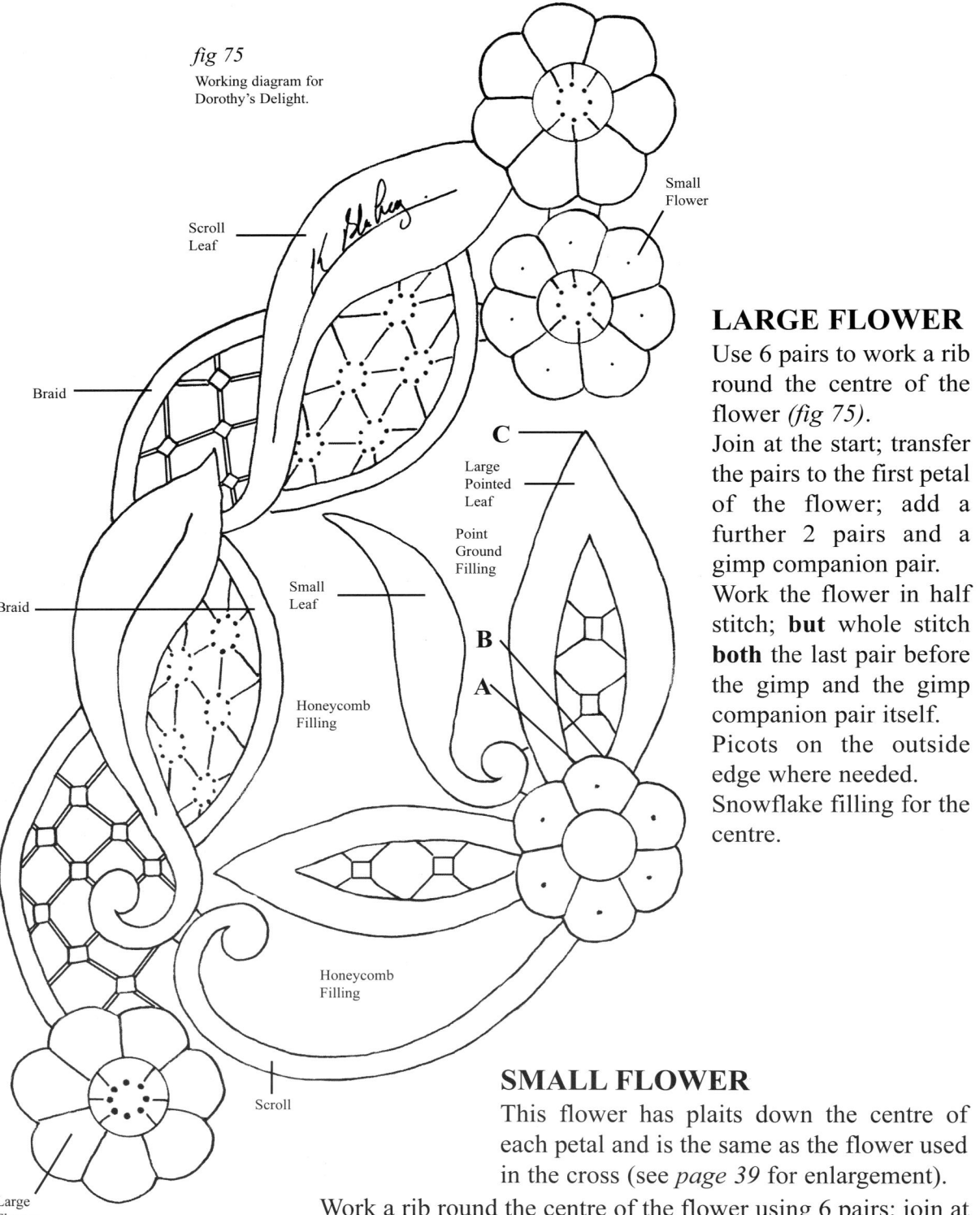

fig 75
Working diagram for
Dorothy's Delight.

Small
Flower

Scroll
Leaf

Braid

C

Large
Pointed
Leaf

Point
Ground
Filling

Braid

Small
Leaf

B

A

Honeycomb
Filling

Honeycomb
Filling

Scroll

Large
Flower

LARGE FLOWER

Use 6 pairs to work a rib round the centre of the flower *(fig 75)*.

Join at the start; transfer the pairs to the first petal of the flower; add a further 2 pairs and a gimp companion pair.

Work the flower in half stitch; **but** whole stitch **both** the last pair before the gimp and the gimp companion pair itself.

Picots on the outside edge where needed.

Snowflake filling for the centre.

SMALL FLOWER

This flower has plaits down the centre of each petal and is the same as the flower used in the cross (see *page 39* for enlargement).

Work a rib round the centre of the flower using 6 pairs; join at the start; transfer to first petal; add a gimp companion pair.

This flower has a small half stitch plait down the centre of each petal: work in half stitch until you reach the centre of the petal; from the outside edge work through the gimp companion pair and the next pair to it; with the next pair work a half stitch; pin; make a plait down the centre; sew in. Take the 2 pairs that were not worked and lay them over the top of the plait; with the pair that was sewn in work back through all the pairs in half stitch.

Continue in half stitch, making the division for each petal. Each petal is worked using the same method. Complete the flower. Work a snowflake filling for the centre.

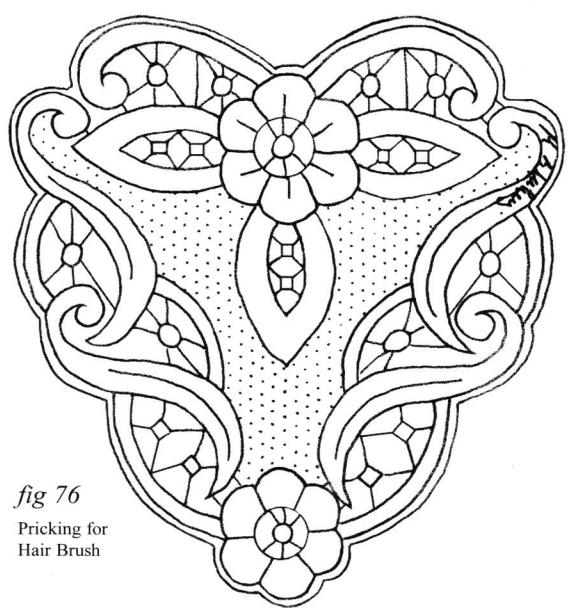

fig 76
Pricking for
Hair Brush

SCROLL

Use 8 pairs plus a double gimp companion pair to make a scroll start. Work the scroll in whole stitch, with a twist after the gimp companion pair. Sew out into small flower.

SCROLL LEAF

Make a point start using 8 pairs and a double gimp companion pair. Work in half stitch increasing pairs to 12 including the double gimp companion pair. A whole stitch vein is worked down the centre of the leaf with 2 pairs.

As the leaf narrows, reduce to 8 pairs; change to whole stitch; continue down the stem finishing with a scroll finish.

Each leaf is worked using the same method.

CLOTHES BRUSH IN HONITON LACE

HONITON FILLINGS
Daisy
No Pin

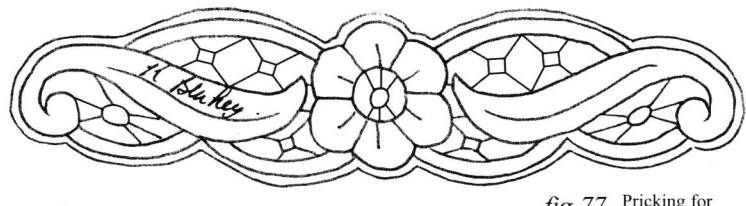

fig 77 Pricking for
Clothes Brush

SMALL LEAF

Make a point start with 6 pairs and a double gimp companion pair. Work the leaf in half stitch, changing to whole stitch upon reaching the stem; finish with a scroll *(page 10)*. Repeat for remaining leaves.

BRAIDS

The braids are are all worked in whole stitch using 6 pairs and a double gimp companion pair. The outside braids have a twist after the gimp, which is on the outside of the braid. The inside braids in the tray are worked in whole stitch only, without the twist after the gimp pair.

In the small designs the braids are the same both inside and out.

fig 78
Pricking for
Powder Bowl

61

POWDER BOWL

LARGE POINTED LEAF

Sew into small flower with 6 pairs at **A**; rib round the centre of the petal; sew out at the other side, at **B**.

With 8 pairs and a double gimp companion pair, make a point start at **C**, working in whole stitch and increasing to 12 pairs, including the double gimp companion pairs. Continue in whole stitch until you reach the centre; divide, giving 6 pairs for each side.

Work down each side in whole stitch, sewing out into the flower.

Finish with a tally down the centre of the leaf.

Repeat for each pointed leaf.

FILLINGS

The fillings on the outside spaces are in whole stitch block.

The inside fillings of the braids are snowflake.

Point ground filling round the centre large petal.

The honeycomb filling (Bucks grid) is worked as [half stitch, pin, half stitch and twist] to give a slightly softer finish.

HAIR BRUSH

fig 79

Pricking for
Hand Mirror

62

fig 80

Pricking for Dressing
Table Tray

The picture of the
Tray may be found on
the back cover.

BIBLIOGRAPHY

JANE NEWBLE-DE GRAAF, Duchesse Lace, Batsford, 1989
CHRISTINE HAWKEN, 121 Honiton Lace Fillings, The Elviston Press, 1997
CAROLINE & BARRY BIGGINS, New Patterns in Honiton Lace, Batsford, 1993
PAT PERRYMAN & CYNTHIA VOYSEY, New Designs in Honiton Lace, Batsford, 1984
DOREEN HOLMES, Flowers in Needlepoint Lace, Batsford, 1987
DOREEN HOLMES, Needlepoint Lace - Designs from the Countryside, Batsford, 1991
CATHERINE BARLEY, Needlelace - Designs & Techniques, Classic & Contemporary, Batsford, 1993
MARY SHIELDS, Lasadoireacht, Wee-Hills Publishing, 1992
MARY SHIELDS, Lasadoireacht II, Wee-Hills Publishing, 1995
YVONNE SCHEELE-KERKHOF, 50 Dutch Bobbin Lace Patterns, Withof & Duchesse, Batsford, 1997
NENIA LOVESEY, The Technique of Needlepoint Lace, Batsford, 1980
NELLIE O'CLEIRIGH, Carrickmacross Lace, Dryad Press, 1985
NELLIE O'CLEIRIGH & VERONICA ROWE, Limerick Lace, Colin Smythe, 1995

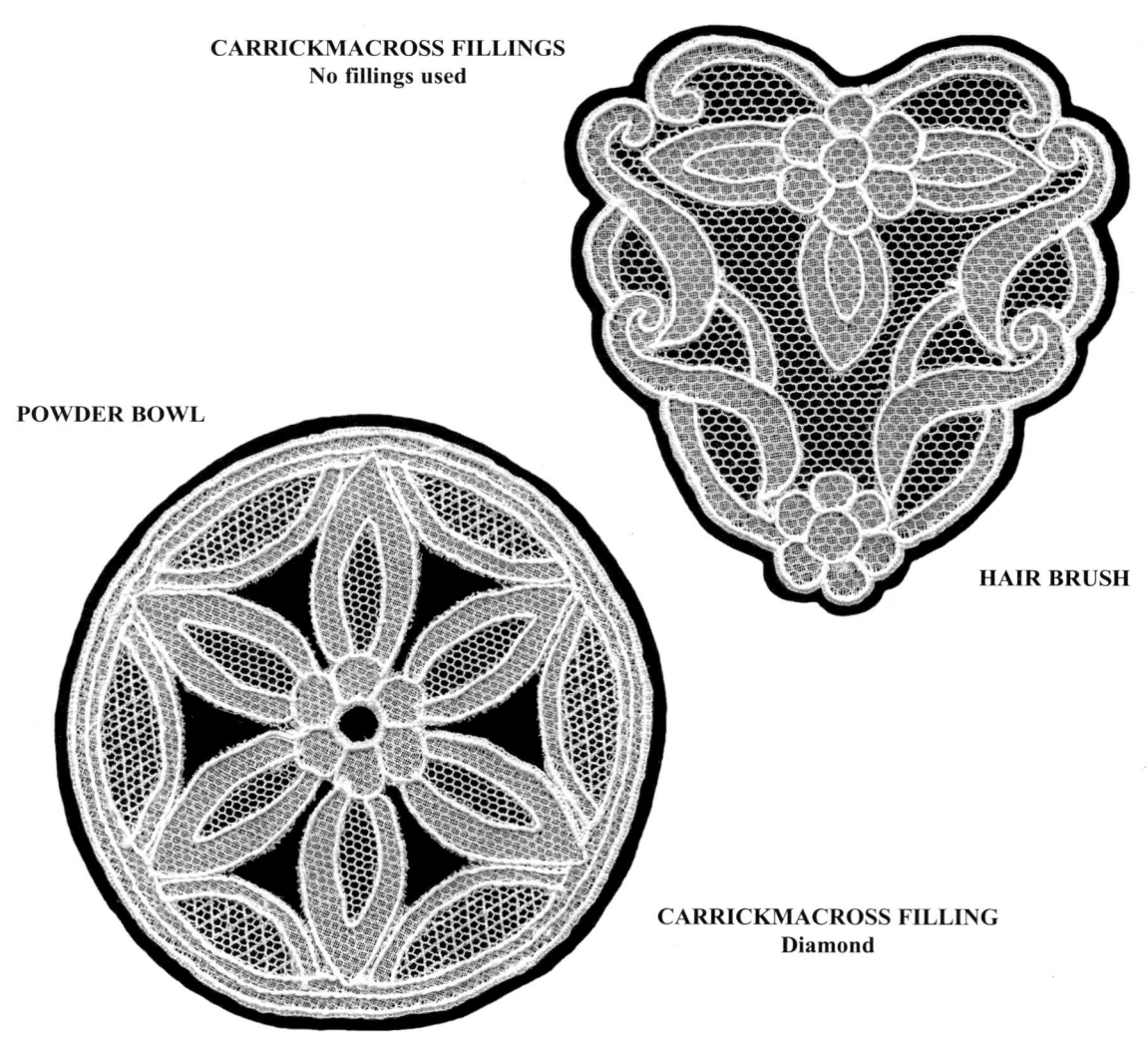

CARRICKMACROSS FILLINGS
No fillings used

POWDER BOWL

HAIR BRUSH

CARRICKMACROSS FILLING
Diamond